DON'T FORGET THE
HOLY SPIRIT

First published in 2023 by
New Life Publishing
Luton, Bedfordshire
reprinted 2023

© Matthew Anscombe

British Library Cataloguing in Publication Data
A catalogue record for this book is available
from the British Library

ISBN   9781912237425

Typesetting by Goodnews Books, Luton UK
www.goodnewsbooks.co.uk
Printed and bound in Great Britain

DON'T FORGET the HOLY SPIRIT

Personal Reflections on Baptism in The Holy Spirit

Matt Anscombe

CONTENTS

For my parents
and in memory of
my sister, Sarah

Foreword

When Fr. Matt Anscombe contacted me recently to tell me he had felt called to write a book on the Holy Spirit, I was honoured that he asked if I would consider writing the Foreword and happily agreed. In due course the printed text arrived by post from Gerard Pomfret of Goodnews Books, the publishers, and I was excited to discover that Matt delivers powerful teaching in every chapter, all based on his own spiritual journey following his personal embrace of baptism in the Holy Spirit.

Matt is a great writer who shares his spiritual journey inspired by the Holy Spirit in a highly acceptable way, maintaining the reader's interest at the highest level on every page, whilst giving top quality teaching, encouragement, and spiritual challenges. I will be happily recommending *Don't Forget the Holy Spirit* to everyone who wants to grow in their relationship with the Father, with Jesus, and of course particularly with the Holy Spirit.

It should not therefore come as a surprise when I tell you that when I sat down with a cup of coffee and picked up the printed manuscript to have a preliminary glance through the book, it was several hours and twenty-seven chapters later before I put it down and got up from my seat. It's a brilliant book! I don't remember ever reading a book from cover to cover without a break. But this one is very special and clearly totally inspired by the Holy Spirit and the author's personal experience.

Matt's personal spiritual journey is fascinating, with the key moment being his experience of baptism in the Holy Spirit which took place at the same time as he felt called to the priesthood, and to which he refers frequently throughout the book. There is so much spiritual and practical wisdom in its twenty-seven chapters that I hesitate to single out any specific examples from a life given to following the leading of the Spirit day by day. Behind it all he simply reminds us in these words from chapter 27, that when we are following Jesus and drawing closer to him, it is the work of the Holy Spirit who is making it happen:

> I simply want to make the point that, when we follow Jesus and draw close, it is the Holy Spirit who is making it happen. The Holy Spirit whom Jesus with the Father sent out across the whole earth and throughout the universe. The Holy Spirit is the fulness of God. There is always more. We need to allow the graces of our Baptism and Confirmation to be released within us so that we can more confidently stand up and proclaim that Jesus is Lord.

Matt's wish-list for parishes at the end of the book is inspiring - read it and then echo his words:

Surely this wish-list is simply God's wish for all his children. This is who we are, and we just need the help of the Holy Spirit to come to know God's promise for us fully.

The combination of Matt's personal experience of living life in the Spirit with its constant and powerful growth, is communicated to the reader on every page of this important book to great effect. I am delighted to recommend it to anyone who is looking for ways to grow and develop spiritually in the midst of a busy life. The great joy is that it is both easy to read and spiritually stimulating, and I am sure it will have a powerful effect on the life of everyone who comes across it or to whom it is recommended. If you are now going to start reading the Introduction, let me assure you that you have made an excellent decision and are about to start a very special and inspirational experience.

Charles Whitehead KSG

Introduction

I believe in the Holy Spirit, the Lord, the giver of life,
who proceeds from the Father and the Son,
who with the Father and the Son is adored and glorified,
who has spoken through the prophets.
(Nicene Creed)

'Don't Forget the Holy Spirit'. Those are the words that came to me when I wondered what title I should give my book. The Holy Spirit had put it on my heart in a flash that I should write a book. 'Just do it' was the confirmation. But why the title?

It has often been acknowledged that the Holy Spirit is like the forgotten Person of the Holy Trinity. We often find it tricky to speak about the Holy Spirit. The Holy Spirit has no face. We can somehow picture the Father through art, even if he is an old man with a fluffy beard! As for Jesus, well he was human. True God and true man, he was like us in all things but sin. He is truly the face of God for us. The Holy Spirit, on the other hand, is variously represented as water, wind or fire. It's somehow difficult to grasp these elements. Yet the Holy Spirit is one with the Father and the Son. The Holy Spirit is Christ's greatest gift to the apostles and thus to the whole People of God.

The role of the Holy Spirit must never be underestimated. The Holy Spirit is the soul of the Church bringing life and unity. The Holy Spirit brings an essential dynamism and is the vital source of the Church's activity. The Holy Spirit renews and rejuvenates. The Holy Spirit is at the heart of the liturgy; the Holy Spirit pours gifts out on the People of God and helps us to follow Christ and proclaim him to the world.

AN ENCOURAGEMENT TO BE OPEN TO BAPTISM IN THE HOLY SPIRIT

For well over twenty years now I have stumbled along the path of discipleship. Eight of these years have been in formation both in religious life and for diocesan priesthood. For the past thirteen I have ministered as a priest within parishes of the Clifton Diocese.

I use the word 'stumble' because, whilst I feel the closeness of Jesus, am sure in my vocation, and regularly sense the Holy Spirit's promptings, power and consolation, these are profoundly challenging times. The look and feel of our parishes have changed, and all too often we are very slow in responding. Those famous words about maintenance of existing structures taking too much priority over mission ring in my ears. Living out diocesan priesthood is, perhaps, the most difficult it has been in the modern era. Also, I am only human and, whilst I serve willingly in the vineyard, I have my own baggage to deal with just like anyone else. I wouldn't want to pretend it's all a bed of roses, even if there is plenty of sweetness and delight.

Nevertheless, I believe the Holy Spirit is urging me to write this book. As I will explain in Chapter 1, my meeting with Christ and my call to priesthood came from the acknowledgment of the Holy Spirit's guidance. I was baptised in the Holy Spirit. As a result, I have often had a profound awareness of the action of the Holy Spirit and understand that this is not everyone's experience, although it can be. I have had people refer to me as 'The Holy Spirit Priest'. When I've asked why they have called me that, they've simply responded that I preach and teach about the Holy Spirit a lot. It is a compliment, and I am humbled by it.

It is with trepidation that I share these thoughts and speak of my experiences. I am not a scholar and in no way is this a theological treatise. It is simply what the Holy Spirit is asking me to share.

The first seven chapters of this book are purely autobiographical. The remainder of the chapters are my own reflections on different aspects of the Christian life with regard to the Holy Spirit. My desire is for people to be open to baptism in the Holy Spirit; to be open to more of the Holy Spirit; to be open to the Holy Spirit's gifts; to have confidence in stepping out in the power of the Holy Spirit; to experience the fruits of the Holy Spirit.

I recognise that every person's journey is different. Many Christians are fully alive in the Holy Spirit and that has come about in myriad ways. It doesn't all have to happen with a 'bang' as it did for me. What I encourage in this book is an honest reflection of where you are in your faith journey. Be open to new possibilities. There is such a great gift in Jesus and his gift to us is his Holy Spirit. Let's allow that gift to come alive in us. Remember the words of Jesus before we begin:

> *'I have come that they may have life and have it abundantly' (John 10:10)*

These are just a few areas in my life that I want to reflect on, and what I have seen in the lives of others.

I offer some reflection questions at the end of each chapter along with Scripture references and other sources. These could be for personal or group reflection. I hope you find these helpful. I've even thrown in a few references to worship songs which I've appreciated over the years. You will find these easily on the internet along with lyrics. I love praise as you'll find out.

THANKS
I want to thank my mum and dad for all their support. They are the ones who first brought me to the Church, handing on the gift of faith and I love them so much.

Thank you to Caroline, who understands me and where I'm coming from. Together we are stronger. Thank you to all our parishioners for your love, devotion and support of my ministry.

Thanks to Charles Whitehead for his support of this book and to Toni and Gerard from Goodnews Books for taking on this project and for their patience with me in this process, as a new and excited author.

Let's crack on with the main event. Remember - all too often the Holy Spirit has been forgotten, but I urge you:

'Don't forget the Holy Spirit'

1

Jesus is Lord

'Therefore I want you to understand that no-one speaking by the Spirit of God ever says 'Let Jesus be cursed!' and no one can say 'Jesus is Lord' except by the Holy Spirit.'
1 Corinthians 12:3

LOST AND FOUND – THE CHILD

Getting lost is a frightening experience. Being a child and suddenly finding that the parent, or parents, that you are with are not there. It brings on a feeling of terror. A slide into a temporary abyss; an indescribable infant despondency. Somehow I can recall that scenario and sense something of the fear. Or, perhaps, it's just that, like most of us, we've seen it happen many times. Mum pushing the trolley down the busy aisle of the supermarket and the two-year old me toddling around paying more attention at low level – little children aren't called 'ankle-biters' for nothing – focusing on the pallet of sugar and split bags and crunching sounds underfoot. Then, suddenly, looking up and realising the safety blanket has gone – 'Where's mum'? Okay, it's probably not a direct thought at that age, rather an instinctive inner reaction.

Desperation sets in, for reason and logic have not yet been

learned. Tears quickly flow. Screams don't take long to follow. It might only be for a minute that she has been distracted, but the sense of time doesn't have much meaning at that age. It could have been an hour!

Then she's there. Then she's there.
Lost, now found.
Terror slips away.
Equilibrium is restored.
'I told you not to go wandering off'. Whatever that may mean.
Everything is going to be okay.
Pure relief.

The experience of being lost and found as a child is very black and white. It's a physical state. One minute they're there and the next minute they're gone. PANIC. Then they're back again. RELIEF.

LOST AND FOUND – THE ADULT
As we get older this experience of being lost and found tends to take on a different meaning. Whilst we may get physically lost, it is often the case that our 'lostness' is an existential or spiritual crisis. It's more about finding meaning and purpose rather than finding comfort in each other. We find ourselves drifting, alienated from ourselves and others, aware that there is something missing. Nothing really seems to satisfy. What can fill that emptiness within? The pain of loss is sharpened, especially when something within seems to want to give the answer and yet, how do we hear it?

ON THE PRECIPICE

It is within this latter context of being lost that my story starts. It was January 2000. I was 28 years old. I was lost. I was frightened. I kept the company of others who seemed equally lost. In fact, I saw in the Millennium in a very dismal fashion. Depression was knocking on the door. A slide towards annihilation haunted me. The vultures were circling. Is that a bit melodramatic? No, not really. I had never considered taking my own life but I genuinely could not see what would bring meaning and contentment. I was on the precipice or staring into the abyss – it's all the same.

It's not as if I'd had a troubled upbringing. I was privileged to have a sound family background. Yes, there was some dysfunction insofar as my middle sister, who died in 1989 at the age of 21, had a lot of health problems and required a lot of attention. That was difficult. Also, my dad, when I was in my early teens worked abroad for two years and I know that had an effect on me in those formative years. What family doesn't have its complications? On the whole we were very fortunate.

The thing with me is that I never really knew what I wanted to do with my life. I can safely say now that I really didn't know myself. I drifted into university and drifted out with a degree. I drifted into sales jobs, having the seeming luxury of being able to travel abroad in export sales – foreign business trips really are just hotels, exhibitions and conference rooms and a passport full of fancy stamps and visas. I found myself at a crisis point at the end of 1999 because I was uncomfortable with the mercenary business motives of my boss. 'It's my way or the highway' he said, in those or similar words. I hadn't realised it, but there was some kind of ethical code within me. I need to find a career better suited to me, I thought – something that gives back to others – but I was lost.

One of the most frightening aspects of being lost was the repeated thought that one possible solution might not be a solution at all. I had hoped that I would find the right partner and that I would get married. What really scared me was the thought that, even if the 'perfect' woman for me came along, there might still be this hole within. That was a genuinely petrifying thought.

FAITH – NEAR BUT FAR?

So where does faith come into all of this? Strangely faith wasn't far away because, having been brought up in a Roman Catholic family, my parents still practised their faith. My dad had been ordained a permanent deacon in July 1999. I, on the other hand, would only occasionally go to Mass if at home at Christmas, but even that wasn't guaranteed. I was quite clear that belief in God made more sense to me than not but, as for Jesus, he was nothing more than an inspired teacher. Was God interested in my life? I didn't think so. God is distant, I thought, not closer to me than I am to myself.

It's worth saying here that my experience of parish, as a

13- or 14-year-old, was not a positive one! I felt the parish priest, a rather short, sulky, fiery old Irishman used to lambast the congregation. It irked me. Perhaps those who were older and wiser let it wash over them. As my dad would say, 'He was admonishing the congregation for the sins of the world'. But for me, it made me angry. It was as if something within me was saying, 'No, this is not right'. Was there already a sense of something to be revealed later?

EPIPHANY 2000
So what was it that made me turn up at Mass at St Mary's Church in Swindon on Thursday 6th January 2000? Or, with the theme of this book in mind, who prompted me to turn up for Mass on that beautiful Feast Day?

Within the context of the confusion and anxiety of my life at that time there was, within me, some desire to be in a place of comfort. Not that I would have been able to articulate this. The Holy Spirit, the Comforter, was reminding me that the People of God gathered together was once, for me, a place of comfort when I was much younger. This is where I needed to be at this time. I had got to a low enough place to realise that I needed to reach out to God. What I was unaware of was God's reaching out to me.

Going to Mass that evening wasn't a moment of epiphany insofar as Christ was not suddenly revealed to me as light to the nations. Being there that evening, though, seemed to allow the Holy Spirit to start some serious work on me. I came out of Mass resolved to want to go to Holy Communion. Was there some deep, hidden sense of respect in me that made me want to absent myself from the Sacrament down through the years? Was I aware of the holiness of this Sacrament, and hence did not approach it as I had clearly chosen not to engage with faith?

It was now, though, that I felt I wanted to be spiritually connected. I wanted to go to Holy Communion and, in order to do so, I would go to Confession that weekend. Surely that was and still is the right way.

It's amazing, or should I say worrying, how the enemy likes to get in at times like this (see Chapter 7). There was a sense in me that I was being drawn to God, and reconciliation would open the way further. Being drawn by God was bringing me hope and consolation, a sense of new life and purpose, and thus a thought came to my mind, 'Everything's going to be okay, you don't need to go to Church'. Immediately my reaction was, 'Get behind me Satan!' I mean, where did that come from? This was the super-powerful work of the Holy Spirit going on within me without my ability to express it. I often wonder what would have happened if I hadn't gone to Confession that day. I know we say that, 'God writes straight with crooked lines', but the Holy Spirit's rebuke, through me, of that thought of the father of lies sometimes makes me wonder what might have been.

RECONCILIATION AND HOLY COMMUNION

Going to Confession was not difficult, but it had probably been 16 or 17 years since I had last gone. At that time I admit that I was unable to make a good examination of conscience, but my honesty in seeking forgiveness was more than sufficient. It is then that the Holy Spirit really seemed to propel me forward.

Straight after Confession I went to Mass and, as I came to receive Holy Communion for the first time in well over ten years, I was given the grace to believe that I was receiving the Body and Blood of Christ. It was as if my 'Amen' to the words, 'The Body of Christ' was really heartfelt in a way I had never experienced before. This was a meeting with Jesus, for sure, but not like the one that would come with power in a few days' time.

It was after receiving Holy Communion that I knelt down in the pew and, somehow, cried out in my heart, 'Lord, show me what I should do with my life'. As I prayed this prayer, I firmly believed that God would show me. This, I still believe to this day, was my first real heartfelt prayer, made with the gift of faith which only the Holy Spirit bestows.

Life was changing. Hope was increasing. Something was afoot. But what? Come Holy Spirit!

LOCKED UP GRIEF

On reflection, during this time, the Holy Spirit was softening my heart and helping me to work on something which would unlock the wellsprings – grief. As I mentioned my sister, Sarah, died suddenly at the age of 21. I question, as a family, whether we really grieved properly. It would have been difficult as my eldest sister lived away and I, the youngest, was 18 and probably not that easy to engage with. In fairness to my parents, who can ever say they get something like this right, as it seems to go against the natural order of things. In spite of my seeming lack of faith, I believed my sister's death was a merciful release and also believed she was in a better place. There was, however, a lot of locked up grief. At this time in 2000, in this graced space which I was not fully aware of, I was able to talk to my parents about my sister. We opened up the photo albums again, read the letters of condolence for a much-loved, faith-filled young woman. I was able to shed tears which I hadn't shed before and I think the groundwork was laid for a revelation.

JESUS IS LORD

I can still vividly remember where it all happened. That little flat in Swindon, with a light and homely lounge. My blue sofas with orange and yellow cushions and a small dining table in the corner. It was at that table that I sat to write a letter to someone whom I had neglected to contact over Christmas due to my own self-obsession. This man was a seminarian whom I had met around the time of my dad's ordination to the Permanent Diaconate and who had listened to my story. Now that things were lightening up in my life, it seemed an appropriate time to write to this man for whom faith was an important part of his life.

'I'm sorry I haven't been in touch', I wrote. 'By the way, I've started going back to Church, and I feel like the Holy Spirit is guiding me'.

WOW! That was it. Never before had I spoken of the Holy Spirit. Never before had I uttered 'Holy Spirit' unless in the context of blessing myself. As soon as I said those words, BANG! I was utterly filled from within. There was an explosion within me that filled me from head to toe with some indescribable power and consolation. It was instantaneous and a word shot up from the core of my being and hit me between the eyes. The word was 'PRIESTHOOD' and at the same time 'YOU SHALL BE A PRIEST'. At this precise moment I met Jesus Christ. Jesus became absolutely real to me as one person to another, except this person was Lord of all Creation, King of Kings, Master, Friend.

The profundity of this moment can never be under-estimated. I knew in an instant that I was loved, that all would be well, that life would never be the same again. As I write this, I cannot help but well up because this was the moment the Father came out to greet me and embrace me. This was the moment Jesus showed me the face of the living God. This was the moment that the Holy Spirit flooded me with divine love. It happened in an instant, in a compressed moment, and from then on there was no going back.

Let us eat and celebrate
for this son of mine was dead and is alive again,
he was lost and is found! (Luke 15:22-24)

Unbound, unburdened, liberated.
Enlightened, empowered, infused.
Called, gifted, cherished.

Twenty years on I told my story on the feast of the Epiphany
in a new parish that I had been asked to minister to.
Personal witness is so important and I got a really positive
reaction to it. One man approached me, though. 'I don't
believe a word of it', he said. Nothing like parishioners to
bring you down to earth!

BAPTISED IN THE HOLY SPIRIT

There are so many words to describe this foundational
moment in my story. The action of the Holy Spirit has always
seemed so dominant to me. I will always remember, and
am meant to remember, that it is at the acknowledgment
of God the Holy Spirit's action, that everything else kicked
off. This is why the Holy Spirit has prompted me to write this
book. The Holy Spirit brings an essential dynamism to our
faith.

What I didn't realise had happened to me in this
fundamental experience was that I had been 'baptised in
the Holy Spirit'. Incredibly, as soon as all of this had
happened, I recognised that the Holy Spirit given to me at
my Baptism and the gifts conferred on me at Confirmation

had just come alive in me. Without recourse to any books, or without any catechesis since the age of 10, I just knew this. What I didn't know was that this phenomenon had a title, and is something that all Christians should aspire to. I explore this in Chapter 5.

FOR REFLECTION & DISCUSSION

At the start of this journey. What is your experience of the Holy Spirit? Do you sense that the graces of your Baptism and Confirmation could be further released in you? Are you open to something new and fresh happening in you?

Who is Jesus for you?

Can you relate to being lost and found?

What is your story?

Is there the possibility that locked up grief holds you back?

Take a look at the parable of the Prodigal Son (Luke 15: 11-32) and meditate on it.

Song: *Love Overcomes* by Jesus Culture featuring Derek Johnson

2

Spirit-Filled
Eucharist

'I will pour out my spirit on all flesh,
your sons and your daughters shall prophesy,
your old men shall dream dreams
and your young men shall see visions.
Even on the male and female slaves,
in those days, I will pour out my Spirit.'
Joel 2: 28-29

A VISION OF THE HOLY SPIRIT

Shortly after my epiphany, as described in Chapter 1, in which Jesus was revealed to me as Lord and Saviour, and the Father's love made known to me by acknowledgment of the Holy Spirit - that eternal moment compressed into a split second, the blink of an eye, I had another profound encounter. This was a gift from The Gift that keeps on giving. It was, for me, a confirmatory sign of my calling towards priesthood, of that I'm sure. It was also a vision of the reality at the heart of the Mass – the pouring out of the Holy Spirit from the Father and the Son over the gifts of bread and wine, and the making present of Christ's sacrifice perpetually offered to the Father in the Holy Spirit.

It would have been a Saturday morning, probably the Saturday memorial of the Blessed Virgin Mary – she who could tell us all a thing or two about the Holy Spirit! I was somewhere near the back of the church, like a good Catholic boy! I have no recollection of the readings that day. All I do recollect very vividly was that during the Eucharistic Prayer I had my head bowed but looked up at the epiclesis – the moment when the priest gently brings his hands together and places them over the gifts of bread and wine. I don't remember hearing the words invoking the Father and Son to send the Holy Spirit, but what I saw seemed to happen in slow motion.

From the hands of the priest there was a kind of heat haze. Emanating from the hands, it covered the central section of the altar, and within this shimmering vision there was a powerful rushing of energy. It was nothing static. It was dynamic. A mighty rushing of power. I knew in my heart that this was the Holy Spirit being poured out.

DREAMING OF THE HOLY SPIRIT
I just took it in. It happened. Time seemed to stand still so that I could take it in, so that the Holy Spirit could impress it upon my mind and heart. Like so many times in life, I quickly moved from the sublime to the ridiculous. After Mass, I got into my car and drove an hour and a half to visit my grandfather (not that I am suggesting visiting my grandfather was ridiculous – but you get the point). Amazingly, although I speak of the Holy Spirit impressing this upon my heart and mind, that image left me for the rest of the day. It didn't come back to mind. That night, however, I dreamt vividly of it. The Holy Spirit really seared

the image of joined hands over the altar with power rushing down into my being in that dream. I would never forget this.

A PRIEST'S WISDOM FROM THE HOLY SPIRIT

I'm very grateful for my parish priest at that time, Fr Liam (now Mgr) Slattery. He was and still is a very zealous priest. I had already spoken to him about my powerful Spirit-filled experiences and my sense of calling. I had shared my feeling of great unworthiness in the face of it all and he had spoken words of great encouragement. Bear in mind, this was all new to me. It had all come out of the blue.

It was with some trepidation that I shared a few days later what I saw that morning, at Mass, with Fr Liam. 'He'll think I'm bonkers', I thought to myself. 'He'll dismiss it out of hand', surely. I needed to share it, though, and his response, as I reflect now, was that of a man totally in accord with the Holy Spirit.

'I saw an almighty power rushing down over the gifts of bread and wine as you celebrated Mass', I told him. 'Well, wouldn't it just take an almighty power to change bread and wine into the Body and Blood of Christ?' he replied in his Irish lilt.

Wow! He had the power to make or break me in that moment. However, true to the priesthood of Jesus Christ, he spoke the words of Jesus, full of Spirit and life.

TO SHARE OR NOT TO SHARE?

Following that grace-filled encounter, where the Holy Spirit was clearly showing me something about the centrality of the Mass and the Spirit-filled encounter with Jesus in his Body and Blood, I rarely shared this story. It's not that I was embarrassed about it – far from it. I was more worried about being misunderstood. I was concerned that people might think I was either potty, or just showing off. To this end, I make reference in Chapter 24 for a very real need for good formation for seminarians, trainee deacons, lay pastoral assistants and catechists when it comes to the Holy Spirit. I certainly never had any and that is very sad. In the fullness of time though, I realised that this vision was, like so many, not just for my edification but was to be shared for the upbuilding of others. I was yet to understand this dimension of what the Holy Spirit was doing.

ORDINATION AND THE HOLY SPIRIT

On the day of my Ordination to the Priesthood, Saturday 17th July 2010, I produced some prayer cards as per tradition. I decided to do something a little different and used an image from Elizabeth Wang (www.radiantlight .org.uk). Her paintings are very much catechetical. They have titles which seek to teach something about the Catholic faith. The picture I chose was entitled, *At Mass we pray with Christ who reaches out to the Father in the burning love of the Holy Spirit.* It depicts to the very left of the picture a small image of a priest stood at an altar. The altar and the priest are coloured black. The priest holds aloft a white host. He is stood in a purple background and yet in front of him, covering the majority of the picture, is a radiant orange and yellow dynamic light. A large Christ figure looms above the altar reaching out and into this almighty power. Tongues of flame rush down from this divine place towards the altar.

Wow! I love this. It makes my heart burn and reminds me to sing with great reverence, and appropriate gusto, the doxology at the end of the Eucharistic Prayer:

> *Through Him and with Him and in Him*
> *O God Almighty Father*
> *in the unity of the Holy Spirit*
> *All glory and honour are yours*
> *For ever and ever.*

And would that the people would heartily sing, 'AMEN'!

It fascinates me how I chose this dynamic image when, as I will explain in Chapter 5, I had not really developed a clear understanding of what had happened to me on that evening in January 2000, over ten years prior. I had been unaware of the charismatic dimension of my following of Jesus. I had rarely spoken about the Holy Spirit per se. But here I was with this dynamic Spirit-filled picture that had really spoken to me. I also chose a beautiful chasuble for my Ordination to the Priesthood with gold tongues of flame running down the central orphrey to represent the Holy Spirit's anointing. Was this a preparation for what was to come in my ministry?

REMINDED OF THE HOLY SPIRIT'S ACTION

Once I had been ordained priest, and as I stood at the altar in the cathedral alongside the bishop, I held out my hands for the first time over the gifts of bread and wine. My hands, where they had been anointed with chrism, became very hot. The same happened again when I celebrated Mass for the first time the next day at St Mary's, Swindon. I believe that it was confirmation to me of what had happened to me through the Sacrament of Ordination. I also knew that this was something to be shared.

A reminder of the gift of priesthood.
A reminder of the Father's love and Jesus the one being offered.
A reminder to share the message of this central liturgical mystery of our salvation.
A reminder to not forget the Holy Spirit.

FOR REFLECTION & DISCUSSION

How does the vision of power coming down over the gifts of bread and wine speak to you?

How do you experience Jesus in the Eucharist?

What are your own experiences of Spirit-filled moments?

'At Mass we pray with Christ who reaches out to the Father in the burning love of the Holy Spirit.'
Reflect on that image and discuss.

Song: *Remembrance* by Matt Maher

3

Astounded by
the Word of God

'As Jesus was walking along,
he saw a man called Matthew
sitting at the tax booth and he said to him,
'Follow me!' and he got up and followed him.'
Matthew 9:9

SO MUCH HAPPENING
It was all happening so fast like a whirlwind. A kindly whirlwind that kept me on my feet but was blowing down my defences – as if they hadn't already been blown down. Jesus was very present to me. There was an incredible sense of consolation. The tenderness of the Father embraced me; hence the Holy Spirit was there at every turn. It was still January 2000.

Prayer seemed to be happening very naturally, as I'll share about in the next chapter. I had an upcoming business trip to Japan, which didn't particularly excite me but my new friend Jesus was steering me with the Holy Spirit through that quagmire. All would be well.

WHAT ABOUT THE WORD?
I arrived home one evening from work and realised, despite all that had been going on with the Holy Spirit and

Jesus, I had not once opened the Bible. So I picked it up. Down through the years I had never discarded it. It had just been gathering dust on the bookcase. On reflection, I wonder whether I was a bit like the Ethiopian eunuch who Philip encountered on the journey from Jerusalem to Gaza in Chapter 8 of The Acts of the Apostles (8:26-39). Even before I opened it I might have heard Philip's question, 'Do you understand what you are reading?', and I could surely have replied as the Ethiopian did, 'How can I unless someone guides me?' Never having really opened the Scriptures before meant there was some trepidation. Where do I start? Where do I go to?

JUST OPEN IT!
I simply decided to open the Bible and see where my eyes alighted. Seems a bit dangerous? I wasn't even sitting down. I was stood and just thought, 'Open it and see what happens'. So I did, and it was Matthew's Gospel that fell open and chapter 9, verse 9 that my eyes alighted on. In the Good News Bible that I had, the little sub-title was simply, 'Jesus calls Matthew'. The text is as seen at the beginning of this chapter.

Following the baptism in the Holy Spirit and all its ensuing delights, including the wonderful eucharistic vision, this was another monumental event. WOW! Again I was flooded with the Holy Spirit. Another generous outpouring which seemed to bring a further sense of liberation. Jesus was calling me. All I wanted to do was to praise God. Had Philip been there, he might have encouraged me in the gift of tongues. There was this incredible energy coursing through my veins. I had given up smoking, and the Holy Spirit had lifted a serious addiction from me with ease. I had started to do some mild exercise, but that night I threw my trainers on and ran close to a half marathon praising God in my heart. Thanking God who had rescued me. Lifting high the name of Jesus, I was like Forest Gump with the injection of the Holy Spirit. 'Run Matty, Run'. This was certainly not running away. This was running towards the Father with Jesus at my side, turbo-charged by the Holy Spirit. This was the third and final deeply powerful sign.

THE WORD ALIVE

My experience, as told above, encouraged me to spend more time with the Word of God, although the newness of Christian faith, and my complete lack of formation from the age of about ten, didn't help. What I did find, though, was that the Word was very much alive. This is a very common experience for those who have recently been baptised in the Holy Spirit. Faith comes alive, a black and white picture appears in technicolour. All aspects of faith life take on a vivid exciting dimension. Scripture suddenly comes alive.

Of course, all too often, especially within the Catholic Church, there is still a lack of confidence with engaging with Holy Scripture. The liturgy when we come to Mass is most definitely shot through with the Word of God. When we listen attentively, presuming the reader helps us, it is Jesus Christ himself who speaks to us in the proclaimed

Word. A prayer to the Holy Spirit can open our ears and hearts to what the Blessed Trinity wants to communicate to us. Yet there is something so intimate about cradling the Word of God in our hands and being unafraid to engage. Enthroning the Word of God somewhere in our house is a wonderful witness.

Scripture is the 'Word of God'. The Word is the second Person of the Trinity through whom all things were made. Scripture is Christ. Thus where we meet Christ, the Word of God, we meet the Father and the Holy Spirit. The Catechism speaks of the Holy Spirit as being the 'principal author of Holy Scripture' (CCC 304). So, it's no wonder that with the graces of our Baptism and Confirmation coming to life in us, the Trinitarian dynamism found on every page of the Bible is bound to come alive.

LOVE LETTERS STRAIGHT FROM THE HEART
God tells us in the Letter to the Hebrews that the word is 'alive and active' (Heb 4:12). It is Christ himself who speaks to us and inflames our hearts with the Holy Spirit. He is the one who tells us directly that his words are spirit and life (John 6:63). Jesus' life is one of constant self-gift in the relationship of the Blessed Trinity. This is what we engage with as we spend time with the Word of God.

So, courage. Take heart. There's lots of great resources out there to help this love letter speak straight to your heart. So don't be afraid to hear of the Father's love for you. Let Jesus speak, and – *__don't forget the Holy Spirit.__*

FOR REFLECTION & DISCUSSION

How do you find the Word of God to be 'alive and active'? How has Christ spoken to you through the Scripture?

How do you reverence the Bible in your house?

What are your favourite Bible passages and why?

'Faith comes alive, a black and white picture appears in technicolour. All aspects of faith-life take on a vivid exciting dimension'.
Is this something you want more of?

Song: *Counting On Your Name* by Tim Hughes

4

Knowing Jesus
in Prayer

'Likewise the Spirit helps us in our weakness;
for we do not know how to pray as we ought,
but that very Spirit intercedes
with sighs too deep for words.'
Romans 8:26

BEHOLDING THE BELOVED

As I alluded to in the previous chapter, prayer seemed to be happening fairly naturally during this new and exciting time. Whilst my mind was regularly turned to Jesus with gratitude, I had a great taste to simply sit quietly and be recollected and listen. This was a pleasant surprise and the Holy Spirit is full of surprises, as I had already discovered.

These early times of prayer were like getting to know a lover. I realised this quite quickly as my heart used to beat faster. I had spoken to a friend of the family, a parishioner at St Mary's, about this. 'That's strange', she said. 'Normally your heart would slow down during a time of prayer'. The Holy Spirit quickly reassured me what was going on. When you fall in love you're excited. Being aware of Jesus so close was giving me that same feeling of elation and arousal as looking into the eyes of one's beloved. It reminds me of the Song of Solomon (2:9-11).

My beloved is like a gazelle or a young stag.
Look, there he stands behind our wall, gazing in at
the windows, looking through the lattice.
My beloved speaks to me and says to me:
'Arise, my love, my fair one, and come away; for
now the winter is past, the rain is over and gone.'

These times of prayer were so consoling. Whilst I lived in Swindon, I worked in Cheltenham. Every lunch time I would go to St Gregory's church for a good forty minutes. The silence. The presence. I'd just never known such beautiful mystery. That was a real oasis and I was drinking deeply of the water welling up.

THE HOLY SPIRIT WITHIN
The Holy Spirit opened up a new understanding about prayer at this time. I had come across a book called, 'Opening to God: A Guide to Prayer' by Thomas H. Green, SJ. Whilst I devoured this timeless classic, I realised that so much of what he was saying about helpful techniques to dispose oneself to quiet prayer was already happening. Prayer, in the end, is simple. Brutally simple and natural. We just expose ourselves to God. I knew the Holy Spirit was teaching me and this was confirmed by a beautiful experience.

I was in my car listening to a tape (I sound old now!) of a conference given by Sr. Briege McKenna. I really had no idea who she was but she was talking about prayer. She spoke of how the Holy Spirit is the one praying within us as per the quote at the beginning of the chapter from St Paul's letter to the Romans. She talked about how it is the Holy Spirit within us who cries out, 'Abba, Father' (Galatians 4:6). Wow! As soon as she spoke those words there was an intense wrenching in my heart. It was amazing. It hurt! For a split second I thought I was having a heart attack but I was quickly assured this was an affirmation of the fundamental point just proclaimed. We are temples of the Holy Spirit. The heart is the centre. It was another beautiful revelation never to be forgotten. Every time I hear those incredible words, I'm braced for it to happen again, although it hasn't yet. Once was enough and the experience was to be shared. These experiences of the Holy Spirit are for the benefit of all. As the Catechism puts it so beautifully, the Holy Spirit truly is 'the master and source of prayer.' (CCC2672)

INTOXICATION

The experience of baptism in the Holy Spirit, coupled with an emerging prayer life, with regular time spent with Jesus in the Blessed Sacrament and nourishment from the Word of God, was teaching me so much. What fascinated me was a brand new, turbo-charged appreciation of the fundamental truths of the faith. I had honestly had a fairly poor catechesis growing up but perhaps some drip-feeding over those much younger years had really helped. It seemed more than that, though. I felt that knowledge, awareness and a whole new language had been mysteriously and quickly infused into me. This is what Cardinal Raniero Cantalamessa, Preacher to the

Papal Household, speaks about when he reflects on the early experience of the Church in the Acts of the Apostles. He describes it as 'sober intoxication of the Holy Spirit'. This is the action of God, filling and renewing the heart; enlightening the mind. This is what was happening to me and can happen to all of us. Oh, what a joyful experience.

Yes, it's totally fair to say that what happened to Peter and the other apostles at Pentecost, and the ensuing witness to the crucified and Risen Christ, and the promise of the Holy Spirit for all, was what was happening to me. According to my gifts and call upon my life, this was the same Holy Spirit bringing forgiveness; purification; new vision and a totally fresh heart. All I had to do was be still and be with Jesus - and not forget the Holy Spirit.

FOR REFLECTION & DISCUSSION

How have you come to know Jesus in prayer? Do you want more? Are you invoking the Holy Spirit to enliven this in you?

Read Acts 1-4 and ask the Holy Spirit to enflame your awareness of his dynamic power.

'Prayer, in the end, is simple. Brutally simple and natural. We just expose ourselves to God.'
Discuss.

Song: *Jesus I Need You* by Hillsong

5

Understanding Baptism in the Holy Spirit

'Did you receive the Holy Spirit?'
Acts 19:2

AN INVITATION

'You're Fr Matt, aren't you?' asked the lady at the door of the presbytery at St Peter's, Gloucester. She had come looking to speak to the parish priest.

'Yes, I am', I replied. 'Fr Liam's not around. Can I help?'

'No it's okay', she said, 'But tell me. Will you come to the Life in the Spirit Seminars at Our Lady of Lourdes in Newent during Lent? It starts next week'.

With that, she said her name was Mary, thrust a flyer into my hand, and off she went.

Little did I know what a great exponent of all things of the Holy Spirit Mary was and still is. Little did she know that being faithful to the Holy Spirit in offering me an invitation, she would soon help me see the bigger picture of what had happened to me eleven years prior. Little did she know how I would really come to understand who I am as a Christian, and as a priest, from the invitation.

LIFE IN THE SPIRIT SEMINARS

I had never come across the Life in the Spirit Seminars before, but was immediately attracted to them. I felt it would be a good discipline to engage with a spiritual practice in Lent and so I agreed to go. The Seminars, which run over seven weeks, were being held in the parish church, a lovely little building in a small town on the edge of the Forest of Dean. The priest, whom I had met before, was Fr Aidan Murray, a Salesian. Unbeknown to me he'd had a powerful experience of the Holy Spirit recently and thus was encouraging of all ways that might help people come to a living relationship with Jesus and an awareness of the gifts of the Holy Spirit.

In essence, the Life in the Spirit Seminars are an opportunity for a short, Spirit-filled catechesis that might open people up to a deeper conversion to Christ, giving the permission for the Holy Spirit to work in their lives in a more powerful way. They reflect on God's love; salvation through Jesus Christ; the gift of the Holy Spirit and the promise of new life in that same Spirit. The key moment is the fifth week, where, having been well-prepared, those attending are ministered to and prayer for their baptism in the Holy Spirit is offered.

GOING BACK A STEP:
AN EXPLANATION OF BAPTISM IN THE HOLY SPIRIT

The basic premise is this, without getting overly theological. In Baptism and Confirmation we receive the fullness of the Holy Spirit – of that we are assured. In Baptism we

are purified from sin, be it original or personal sin. We become new creatures in Christ as adopted children of God and we become temples of the Holy Spirit. We become members of the Body of Christ, anointed as priests, prophets and kings. We no longer belong to ourselves but to Christ and the Church, and we are given the power to live and act under the prompting of the Holy Spirit through the gifts of the Holy Spirit.
PLEASE DON'T PASS THAT BY LIGHTLY!

In Confirmation, the effects of the Sacrament are even more closely linked to the Holy Spirit. This is the Pentecost sacrament where, particularly if we were baptised as infants, we get to say 'Yes' to the promises made on our behalf by our parents, guardians and godparents. In Confirmation is brought about a deepening in that bond as true children of God; it unites us more firmly to Christ and it increases the gifts of the Holy Spirit in us.

As we see, the Holy Spirit has been given to us. If we were to be asked the question that St Paul asked to some in Ephesus, 'Did you receive the Holy Spirit?' (Acts 19:2), we would most certainly be able to reply in the affirmative. However, the question may need to be, 'Okay, you've got the Holy Spirit, but has the Holy Spirit got you?' Have you allowed the Holy Spirit to really come alive in you? You see, this was my issue in 2000. I had received the Holy Spirit in full at Baptism and Confirmation but the graces had not flourished. They'd never really been unbound.

I have always liked the analogy of receiving a gift. A friend visits and gives you a lovely box neatly wrapped up. 'Wow! Thank you', you say. You see the box as the gift without realising that if you were to open it you'd find a whole array of wonderful treasures that would enrich your life.

I understand that there will be some reading this who may find this rather one-dimensional. Each has their path of discipleship and many in our parishes are very much alive in the Holy Spirit through different means. I spoke with the Abbot of Douai Abbey about this and he recounted how he was baptised in the Holy Spirit as a boy whilst receiving Holy Communion. He remembers the precise moment and the experience and with it a sudden longing to be a priest. He wouldn't doubt, however, that many need encouragement to bring the graces of our Baptism and Confirmation more alive. Baptism in the Holy Spirit reignites the graces already given, and equips and empowers Christians for mission. That is why the current and previous several Popes have been so in favour of it. It is the goal of the Christian life.

BACK TO THE SEMINARS

The Life in the Spirit seminars were, for me, something of a revelation. It did four things.

♦ Firstly, I went forward for prayer for 'baptism in the Holy Spirit' and certainly know that I received a fresh outpouring; a fresh release of gifts. Let's remember that the Holy Spirit is regularly poured out. In fact, even as I have been reflecting and am writing this account, I am realising more and more that there was a huge amount given to me to really move me on.

♦ Secondly, it made me understand that baptism in the Holy Spirit was what I had experienced in January 2000. For me, naming that was important, alongside the various phenomena that went along with it.

♦ Thirdly, it introduced me to Charismatic Renewal which, sadly, I had never really heard of or experienced in the previous eleven years.

♦ Fourthly, it compelled me to start to explore more and serve this current of grace in the Church, for I felt at home here. Here was the spirituality that I felt most at ease with. The language of the Holy Spirit, the gifts of the Holy Spirit, 'the passion for Jesus', the desire for mission. Dynamite!

CHARISMATIC RENEWAL

What a blessing again to have a supportive, wise parish priest, namely Fr Liam from back in 2000. He could see what the Holy Spirit was doing. He already sensed that my attending the Seminars in Newent would lead to bringing Charismatic Renewal into St Peter's, Gloucester. He'd had his own positive experiences of Catholic Charismatic Renewal (CCR) in his earlier years of priesthood. He could see how starting a prayer group and running Life in the Spirit Seminars would all be in accord with our mission of spreading the Gospel and encouraging faith and Spirit-filled disciples.

There is sometimes a reductive view of CCR – 'Oh, it's all happy-clappy'. That is a terrible disservice to what, as I described it above, is a 'current of grace' in the Church. Okay, one might attend an event run by CCR where the worship music is loud and people are dancing. It might not seem your 'cup of tea'. Ask the Holy Spirit to open your eyes to what is happening. Through the grace of CCR, countless millions have come to be transformed into passionate, committed Christians. Many of our parishes have deeply committed disciples who, at some point, have been baptised in the Holy Spirit through engagement with CCR. They might not be involved with CCR now, but the current of grace helped the Holy Spirit to capture them.

My experience of baptism in the Holy Spirit wasn't directly linked to CCR. If I hadn't been baptised in the Holy Spirit, though, I wouldn't be writing this. If I hadn't accepted that invitation from Mary to the Life in the Spirit Seminars, I wouldn't be able to articulate half of what I am trying to say in this book.

PAT, POPE BENEDICT, AND THE HOLY SPIRIT
We have a beautiful soul, called Pat, in one of our parishes, who is a great advocate for baptism in the Holy Spirit. Whatever issue is brought up at a Parish Pastoral Team

meeting, her solution is always, *'Baptism in the Holy Spirit'*.

'We need more catechists.' *'Baptism in the Holy Spirit is what we need'*, she will say.

'What about catering for the quiz night?' *'Baptism in the Holy Spirit'* will be her offering.

This lady is a prophet because baptism in the Holy Spirit really is an answer to a lot of the flatness in our parishes. In fact, this book is probably coming about because of her re-focusing me on this whole issue.

Let me leave the last words to our dear friend, the late Pope Benedict XVI. Like St John Paul II and Pope Francis, he was a great supporter of Catholic Charismatic Renewal and an advocate for baptism in the Holy Spirit.

Let us discover, dear brothers and sisters, the beauty of being baptised in the Holy Spirit. Let us be aware again of our Baptism and of our Confirmation, sources of grace that are always present.
Pentecost 11 May 2008

No, never forget the Holy Spirit!

FOR REFLECTION & DISCUSSION

Have you forgotten the Holy Spirit?

Reflect on Pope Benedict's quote above? What comes up for you?

Do you understand what is on offer? Are you ready to ask for more?

Song: *Fresh Outpouring* by Jesus Culture featuring Kim Walker-Smith

6

A Passion For Mission

*'Go out to the whole world,
proclaim the Good News
to all creation.'*
Mark 16:15

FILLING IN THE GAPS

I'm conscious of gaps in my story so far – about ten years to be precise! Having spoken to someone in the diocese about vocation to priesthood, there was a suggestion of moving forward quickly. I intuited, though, that I needed a good deal more time. I needed to get out of my current job, which had just taken me on a fascinating trip to Japan and Singapore. A simple, stress-free job would be good. Moving back with my parents for a while was necessary. Most importantly, time was needed for me to go deeper in all things of the Lord.

There was another really powerful Spirit-filled moment at this time. There have only been a couple of times in my life of discipleship where God has clearly commanded me to do something. My closest friend at the time was perplexed by all that was happening for me. My discovery of Jesus and my sudden change of demeanour troubled him. We had planned to go on holiday together to Canada at the end of January. He was becoming unsure about it although I was happy to crack on with the booking. When I asked him if he had booked the package holiday, he said that he had got through to the call centre but the agent on the end of the line just couldn't hear him. It all sounded very strange.

That evening I decided to drop round to his house but, as I parked up outside, I was suddenly very aware that I couldn't get out of the car. I was being held back and then a clear voice said, 'Go to Valladolid'. As I mentioned in chapter 1, I had met a seminarian a few months before. He was studying at the English College in Valladolid. It was as I was writing to him that my baptism in the Holy Spirit occurred.

I am extremely grateful for that clear prompt which flooded me with joy. It was clear that my friend and I needed space from each other. A trip to Canada together would probably have been a bad thing. The Holy Spirit was compelling me to push forward in exploration of priest-hood.

THE REDEMPTORISTS – PLENTIFUL REDEMPTION
One thing is abundantly clear to me now. At that time I really didn't have much idea of what, or who a priest is, or even what a priest does. I also wondered whether it might be a lonely existence, and someone prompted me to consider the idea of community and religious life. It was at that time that my mum and dad invited me to join them

on a retreat at Hawkstone Hall run by the Redemptorists. They had been very impressed by Fr Denis McBride at a recent event and wanted to experience more of his beautifully delivered, erudite, but witty lectures.

I immediately hit it off with the Redemptorists that I met. Their missionary charism really appealed to me. I felt a connection with the way they preached the Gospel. Mission. Mission. Mission. That excited me. I left that retreat with an incredibly strong feeling that I had been led there because that was where the Lord wanted me to be in the future. I was amazed at how the Holy Spirit was making things so clear, even if I wasn't quite using that language.

I feel it is an incredible disservice to the Redemptorists to summarise five very formative years with them in one paragraph. What a privilege to spend a year as a postulant in Edinburgh, to complete a novitiate in Ireland for a full year, which gave me a great grounding. What a grace to go back to Edinburgh and then study for three years at Scotus College in Bearsden, Glasgow, during the week.

Ultimately, though, God called me away from the Redemptorists. In a beautifully-graced moment, the Lord helped me to make the decision to leave. For the time being, I had to surrender the idea of priesthood and jump off the cliff without being concerned about the expectations of others. Without knowing quite what would happen, I had to trust that all would be well. Of course, I knew Jesus now. The parachute would open, the Lord would be by my side, the Holy Spirit would steer me.

DIOCESAN PRIESTHOOD
It wasn't long before I twigged that I was being called to diocesan priesthood within my own diocese, and was encouraged by those I knew in formation to not hang around and procrastinate. 'What about the missionary element?', I thought. 'This is what you are to bring to the diocese', was the Lord's reply. 'A missionary thrust is what you will be all about'. But this would only come once I was more clearly aware of the action of the Holy Spirit.

Unfortunately, in my years with the Redemptorists and latterly with the diocese, the language of the Holy Spirit, the gifts of the Holy Spirit, and the ability to step out in the power of the Risen Lord had not been communicated. It had not been named. Nobody had told me about baptism in the Holy Spirit. In hindsight, with that same Holy Spirit to help me reflect, my journey to that point was my journey. There is a sadness, though, in my opinion, about a definite lack of formation in this area. So it was the Life in the Spirit Seminars in 2011 that would give me that requisite understanding, and the shape and feel of my priesthood and ministry would become clearer and new ventures would follow.

NEW AWAKENINGS
In my time with The Redemptorists, I was fortunate to be able to assist on a few occasions on parish missions,

preached retreats, youth ministry and outreach. I had some brief experience of missionary work in Honduras and had led a mission week in Spanish in a small Mass Centre in the second city of San Pedro Sula.

It was out of the blue, though, that the Holy Spirit put a word on my heart and mind. I was sat in the chapel of the Marist Convent in Nympsfield, on top of the Cotswolds in Gloucestershire. I was with my Jesus Caritas priestly fraternity. Sat there, I gazed on the lovely, colourful, round stained-glass window above the sanctuary. It was an image of the Holy Spirit as a dove descending. As I sat transfixed, the letters 'D M T' came into my head and I immediately assumed that meant Diocesan Mission Team! I shared this inspiration with the group later and Fr Jim Williams, who I hadn't met previously, simply said, 'If you get a team together you can come and do a week-long mission in the five parishes that I help to serve. Surely that was the confirmation I needed, and a team quickly came together and the bishop was supportive of what I was offering.

That mission week took place between Ascension and Pentecost and was a powerful event. It was the first of seven one-week missions offered to parishes in the diocese. It came under the banner of 'New Awakenings', another word placed on my heart. Again, I remember exactly where and when that came to me.

The 'main event' of the week was always the Thursday

night 'healing service' – an opportunity to share my testimony, proclaim Jesus as Lord with great confidence in the power of the kerygma and then offer an invitation: seek reconciliation through Confession and then come forward for prayer for healing and a fresh outpouring of the Holy Spirit.

Seven parish missions might not sound much, but for me it was a joy to be able to offer these alongside my ministry within the parish, and then as Catholic Chaplain to the University of Bristol and Vocations Director for the Diocese. I still meet people from those parishes who remember them with fondness. It's all about sowing seeds.

The parish mission prayer, prayed in preparation for these missions, is one that we have adopted in the South Bristol Mission Area, the four parishes that I minister to. I love the Trinitarian dynamism of this prayer.

> Father, pour out your Holy Spirit upon our parishes to deepen in us a thirst and passion for mission. Grant that your gifts of faith, hope and love will lead us in true discipleship, so that the Good News of Jesus Christ will find a home in our hearts and open us to the needs of all.
>
> Then, trusting in your Almighty power, give us the courage to proclaim our faith in Him to a broken world. Amen

Stepping out in faith on this 'New Awakenings' venture was an eye-opener in many ways, not least for another area that no one had ever really talked to me about. An area never covered in any of my formation years, but something clearly evident in the Word of God. Something which the Holy Spirit makes us very aware of and helps us to deal with. I am speaking about spiritual warfare.

FOR REFLECTION & DISCUSSION

How have you felt the Holy Spirit calling you to share the Good News? What are your experiences of talking about Jesus?

Meditate on Matthew 28:16-20. Imagine you are there. Picture the scene and stay with it quietly. How does this speak to you?

Are you in need of a 'New Awakening'? Are you prepared to ask the Holy Spirit for this?

Song: *Where Would We Be* by Matt Redman

7

Spiritual Warfare

*'Be calm but vigilant because your enemy
the devil is prowling around like a roaring
lion looking for someone to eat.
Stand up to him, strong in faith.'*
1 Peter 5: 8-9

LOVE IS A BATTLEFIELD
Wow! Was I unprepared for some of the opposition I would encounter as I stepped out more in the power of the Holy Spirit!

When we think of warfare, most of us probably picture the tragedy of open armed combat. Tanks, planes, ships, shelling, targeted missiles. Destroyed buildings, boots on the ground, shattered lives. But nowadays there is the more hidden battle of cyber warfare. Targeted attacks by foreign, enemy powers. How much more frightening when you can't see the enemy so very close to you.

DO NOT BE AFRAID
I write this chapter as an encouragement. I think it is vitally important for us to truly own our Christian story. We have an Almighty God who, through Christ's death on the Cross and his glorious Resurrection, has conquered death and

conquered the enemy, so that in the fullness of time all of creation will be in thrall to the triumphant King. However, in these end times, the devil is still very much around. His wish is to thwart goodness at every turn, and our role is to bring the power of Christ to bear over those situations.

What I was finding out, as I planned the first New Awakenings mission, was that the enemy was not happy and, knowing my lack of preparedness, caught me off guard. I realised later that this was all a good sign of what I was doing in my faithfulness to the Holy Spirit's prompting, but it was an unexpected shock.

BATTING OFF THE ATTACK

Firstly, there was a feeling of oppression at night. A feeling of heaviness pressing down from outside. Dreams became full of 'trickster' characters – seemingly demonic in nature. I'm not being naïve here. There was psychological baggage that I needed to deal with, but there was clearly a contrary spirit messing about with that. Fortunately, I had others with experience who could give me good counsel with regard to this.

It is the Holy Spirit who comes to our aid here. The Holy Spirit enables us to call on the name of Jesus. There is such power in the name of Jesus. I hate to hear that beautiful, holy name misused. In these situations we have authority to say, 'Get behind me, Satan!' just as I did when tempted to resist reconciliation in 2000.

I confess at this time to falling into a bit of a trap. With that feeling of oppression in the darkness, I found myself sleeping with a little bit of light on. It comforted me. It was also confirmed by a retreat-giver on a charismatic priests' retreat as something that she did too. But it was a mistake. Christ is our Light! A priest friend reminded me of that, and after requesting some prayer ministry around this whole subject I moved on and never looked back.

THE ARMOUR OF GOD

Many reading this book will have far more experience around this area than I, and will realise that the enemy never fully flees, especially as we move powerfully in the Holy Spirit's anointing. Things become more subtle. Calling on the Holy Spirit for discernment becomes important. For me, there can sometimes be a kind of paralysis – it's a complex area – a good spiritual guide is really necessary. Regular confession is really important.

I cannot recommend highly enough putting on the armour of God. Christ speaks to us, in chapter 6 of Ephesians (6:10-18), about allowing the Holy Spirit to dress us in God's armour. When I have done this by calling on the Lord to dress me with ...

- the helmet of salvation;
- the breastplate of righteousness;
- the belt of truth;
- the shield of faith;
- the gospel shoes of peace;
- the sword of the Spirit;

...I can categorically say that I have felt direct barbs of the enemy bouncing off me. Even in very tangibly Spirit-filled times of ministry, the enemy is at work, but appropriate prayers of protection allow you not to be dragged down but to keep moving forward in the power of the anointing of the Holy Spirit.

THE DANGER OF THE OCCULT

When I was about 13 years old, some school friends decided they were going to play with a Ouija board. I admit that most of my life I would easily give way to peer pressure. However, on this matter, there was something inside (yes, the Holy Spirit, as I realised later) which firmly made me resist this. Wow! How thankful I am for that protection. Those friends of mine said they were scared to death of what happened that night. The boy whose house this took place in said the family were convinced something unfriendly came into that room that night and remained. It was in a new conservatory room at the back of the house and no-one wanted to go in there anymore.

Even though I thought that God was distant in my teens and twenties, matters of the occult were something I kept well away from. Again, I realise now, it's about owning and properly understanding our story. Demonic oppression, demonic infestation – these things happen. Dabbling with the occult is extremely dangerous. Once I had started to step out more in the power of the Holy Spirit, I found cases coming my way. House blessings for deliverance; simple prayers of deliverance for the afflicted. I'm not speaking of solemn exorcisms here. This is an area to be dealt with by a properly appointed diocesan team. Discernment in this area is key and there will be no surprise when I say that it is the Holy Spirit who gives that gift too.

My eyes were really opened on a trip to Uganda, Rwanda and Tanzania in 2014. It was here that I witnessed all sorts of manifestations of evil spirits which any sceptic would find hard to debunk. Lands where witchcraft and traditional religion are still prevalent are bound to be open to such spirits. I was even attacked by a man whilst celebrating Mass. I could see it play out before me. His face seemed to change and he suddenly ran towards me but collapsed to the ground as I put my arm up in resistance.

JESUS AND SATAN

Jesus cast out demons. In doing so he was demonstrating the coming Reign of God, already present in him. This is a difficult subject for many. There is still a certain incredulity. The devil must be loving it. I have heard of priests who don't even believe this. Yes, really! There needs to be proper formation in this area as I allude to in chapter 24. Pope Francis is hot on this subject. He doesn't shy away from the true narrative. This whole realm only became apparent to me with the help of the Holy Spirit. Jesus is victorious. Victorious over sin, death and the devil!

We do not need to be afraid.

Invoke the name of Jesus and don't forget the Holy Spirit.

FOR REFLECTION & DISCUSSION

Some people say that when they come to deepened faith, there are associated voices which seem to come to them telling them not to bother. It never brings peace and is not of God. Have you experienced this before? Discuss this with others.

Read Ephesians 6:10-19 and reflect on the need to put on the armour of God. Discuss how it is the Holy Spirit who dresses us.

Have you ever dabbled with the occult? If so, have you repented of it so that you can be further filled with the Holy Spirit?

Song: *Defender* by Jesus Culture

8

Sharing in Jesus' Anointing

'And just as he was coming up out of the water,
he saw the heavens torn apart and the Spirit
descending like a dove on him. And a voice
came from heaven, 'You are my Son, the Beloved;
with you I am well pleased.'
Mark 1:10-11

THE BAPTISM OF JESUS

What are your favourite Bible images? Which biblical accounts fire your imagination and leave you with a strong picture in your mind. There are so many. Art probably has a strong influence here. Sometimes we can really place ourselves into the scene. I've always loved the scene of the return of the prodigal son - the father a long way off watching for him; the tenderness of the embrace; the rejoicing. Also the journey to Emmaus – downcast disciples feel their hearts begin to burn as this seeming stranger walks alongside them, and then they understand at the breaking of bread; the sense of awe; the expansion of the mind and heart. So many Spirit-filled scenes to contemplate and build us up in the love of Christ, who is the One proclaimed through all Scripture. It is the Holy Spirit who inflames our hearts as we ponder all of these.

There are so many specific accounts of the Holy Spirit to

reflect upon in the pages of the Bible too. The Baptism of Jesus in the Jordan is one which has very powerful imagery. I've often prayerfully imagined this in my mind. Jesus, in humility, approaches John the Baptist. John had already prophesied that the one on whom the Spirit descends is the one who will baptise with the Holy Spirit and fire. John points out Jesus as the Lamb of God. Jesus' baptism is a stepping off point for him; a launch pad for his immediate preparation for his public ministry. Jesus always was one with the Father and the Holy Spirit. This submission to John's baptism brings about a revelation and a specific anointing – a kind of public divine approval; the mandate to move forward and begin to proclaim the Kingdom of God. It is a moment of intimacy which, however the event may have looked at the time, really speaks to the heart.

The description in Mark's Gospel of the heavens being 'torn apart' is reminiscent of theophanies in the Old Testament. These were visible manifestations of God to humans, particularly the prophets. Ezekiel talks about how the heavens were opened and he saw visions of God (Ezk 1:1). Isaiah cries out that the heavens might be torn open and God come down (Isa 64:1). Stephen, after Pentecost, witnessing boldly in the power of the Holy Spirit, gazes into heaven and sees the glory of God (Acts 7:55-56). At Jesus' baptism the heavens are torn open and God reveals who Jesus is, and the divine nature. This moment is somehow an encouragement and empower-ment of Jesus for what lies ahead. It is an anointing of Jesus as the king proclaiming a new kingdom – the reign of God.

It is a revelation of who Jesus is and who the Blessed Trinity is – Father, Son and Holy Spirit.

The profundity of the moment of Jesus' baptism can never be lost on us. However it happened, it is clear that God is making a point about who Jesus is as the anointed one. Jesus is Christ. Jesus was always anointed because the Holy Spirit is his anointing. In this moment, though, it is as if the Holy Spirit, who has always been with Jesus, is activated in a new way for all that lies ahead.

JESUS, THE HOLY SPIRIT AND US
Particularly in Luke's Gospel, we hear how Jesus does everything in the power of the Holy Spirit. This is really important because what Jesus did, in the power of the Holy Spirit, we are able to do too. Immediately after his baptism, we are told that Jesus, 'full of the Holy Spirit', was led by that same Holy Spirit into the wilderness. Jesus was tempted there for forty days (Lk 4:1-12). The assumption here has to be that Jesus fought temptation in the power of the Holy Spirit. This is something that we can do too. We do not do God's work in our own power. Jesus is with us in the Holy Spirit at moments of temptation. He is by our side at times of upbuilding in the wilderness.

Luke again highlights the role of the Holy Spirit as Jesus returns to Nazareth after the forty days in the wilderness. We are told that he was 'filled with the power of the Holy Spirit' (Lk 4:14-19). Jesus refers to his anointing by proclaiming that he is fulfilling the prophesy of Isaiah: 'The Spirit of the Lord is upon me'. Jesus is the one proclaiming the year of the Lord's favour. Restoration is being brought about in him, always in the Holy Spirit's power. He is preaching in the power of the Holy Spirit. We too are filled with this power and can be open to preaching and teaching Jesus in this same power of the Holy Spirit.

The agency of the Holy Spirit seems to be apparent as Jesus heals. We hear that the 'power of the Lord was with him to heal' (Lk 5:17). 'Power' is referred to a lot throughout the New Testament. It is a translation of the Greek word '*dunamis*', which is the root of our English words 'dynamite' and 'dynamic'. This is the kind of dynamism brought about by the Holy Spirit. The disciples were told by Jesus at his Ascension that they would receive '*dunamis*' when the Holy Spirit came upon them (Acts 1:8). Look what happened at Pentecost! We can be open to bring healing to others in Jesus' name in this power of the Holy Spirit. We can be open to receiving healing by the same action of the Holy Spirit.

We also hear how Jesus rejoiced in the Holy Spirit (Lk 10:21). What a beautiful image. Jesus giving verbal thanks and praise to God from his heart. Oh, how we truly desire to give praise to God. This is what we were created for! As one of the Common Prefaces to the Eucharistic Prayer in the Mass states, 'For, although you have no need of our praise, yet our thanksgiving is itself your gift, since our praises add nothing to your greatness but profit us for salvation'. What a gift!

Jesus also talks about the Father desiring to give the Holy Spirit to those who ask (Luke 11:9-13). If only we would ask more. Cry out! He speaks too of the 'finger of God' that he uses to cast out demons (Lk 11:20), another special image of the Holy Spirit. Exorcism is, of course, a gift of the Holy Spirit to be used with appropriate care and discernment (see chapter 7).

REFLECTING ON OUR BAPTISM

In the Letter to the Romans, St Paul describes our baptism into Christ. He says, 'We have been buried with him by baptism into His death, so that, just as Christ was raised from the dead by the glory of the Father, so we too might walk in newness of life' (Rom 6:4). When we were baptised, the celebrant explained in the rite that, through the God of power and Father of the Lord Jesus Christ, we were freed from sin and brought to new life through water and the Holy Spirit. Jesus sanctified the water of baptism through his death and resurrection. The Holy Spirit rushes down to claim those being baptised for Christ. The Holy Spirit anoints; enlightens; clothes with the splendour of Christ. The Holy Spirit makes us temples of that same Holy Spirit.

I have to regularly reflect on the celebration of baptism. Sometimes baptisms can be a bit manic in the parish church! This is a great opportunity to share the Gospel but it can feel quite challenging. Tears, noise, a lack of connectedness to the Church, apathy. These are all things that are around and can feel quite distracting. Many people seek baptism for their children because of an inherent sense of rightness, but there is often a question around faith. In spite of this, the outpouring of the Holy Spirit is assured. Children are not to be denied this grace for with it comes a special investiture at the start of their exciting journey with Jesus. This is why we need to consider what happened to us at our own baptism and how Jesus is with us through this, and how the Holy Spirit graces us and empowers us in the Sacrament. For through this Sacrament we share in Jesus' anointing and, open to the Holy Spirit, who completes this work in us through Confirmation, we can do the things that Jesus did. We resist temptation, preach, teach, heal, cast out demons, praise. We receive gifts in abundance.

PRIESTS, PROPHETS AND KINGS

How important it is for us to remember that we all share in the common priesthood of Jesus Christ through baptism. As I discuss in the next chapter, the gifts of the Holy Spirit are on offer to all, not just for some exclusive elite. We are called to set free the gifts so that we are not passive bystanders in the life of the Church. Priests offer sacrifice and praise and we are all called to do that day in and day out. Prophets speak God's words and are open to proclaiming truth in all areas of their lives. Kings and queens lead and give good example. They encourage others. This is what we are all about through our baptism.

We will now reflect on the gifts of the Holy Spirit, which we all receive in baptism. These are gifts that are also on offer

at particular moments for the building up of the Body of
Christ. Having reflected on our baptism, let us be aware of
the need to fan these gifts into a flame.

FOR REFLECTION & DISCUSSION

Spend some time with Luke's Gospel looking at how
Jesus ministered in the Holy Spirit.

dunamis = power. How are you experiencing that
power of the Holy Spirit at this moment in your life?

When were you baptised and where? What
happened to you that day? Who did you become?

Priest, prophet, king – discuss!

Song: *Anointing* by Jesus Culture

9

Gifts of the
Holy Spirit

*'To each is given the manifestation of the Spirit
for the common good. To one is given through the Spirit
the utterance of wisdom, and to another the utterance
of knowledge according to the same Spirit, to another
faith by the same Spirit, to another gifts of healing by
the one Spirit, to another the working of miracles, to
another prophecy, to another the discernment of
spirits, to another various kinds of tongues, to another
the interpretation of tongues. All these are activated
by one and the same Spirit, who allots to each one
individually just as the Spirit chooses.'*
1 Corinthians 12:7-11

RECEIVING THE HOLY SPIRIT
I was born on 24th March 1971 at Musgrove Park Hospital,
Taunton.
I was baptised on 9th May 1971 at St Joseph's, Bridgwater.
I was confirmed on 9th May 1982 at St Teresa of Lisieux,
Taunton

Naturally, I can't remember the first two events in the
above list but I don't even recall receiving the Sacrament
of Confirmation at the age of 11. I cannot remember a
single preparation class. All I have is a picture of me looking

very smart and kneeling at the altar rail with Bishop Mervyn Alexander putting chrism on my forehead, but I have absolutely no recollection of that event. What I am assured of, though, is that the Holy Spirit was given to me at both my Baptism (see chapter 8) and my Confirmation. This was the prayer that Bishop Mervyn prayed in invocation of the Holy Spirit over me and the other confirmands:

All-powerful God, Father or our Lord Jesus Christ,
by water and the Holy Spirit
you freed your sons and daughters from sin
and gave them new life.
Send your Holy Spirit upon them
to be their helper and guide.
Give them the spirit of wisdom and understanding,
the spirit of right judgement and courage,
the spirit of knowledge and reverence.
Fill them with the spirit of wonder and awe in your
presence. We ask this through Christ our Lord.

We believe that Confirmation unites us more firmly to Christ. It brings an increase and deepening of the grace received at Baptism. It increases the gifts of the Holy Spirit within us. This sacrament, like Baptism, leaves an indelible spiritual mark on us. It completes Baptism by Jesus Christ sealing us with the seal of the Holy Spirit. Wow! That's a lot to unpack.

HELPER AND GUIDE

As I discussed earlier, when I was baptised in the Holy Spirit;

when the gifts of the Holy Spirit truly came alive in me back in 2000, I quickly realised that this flowed from my Baptism and particularly my Confirmation. I quickly became aware that the Holy Spirit had been my helper and guide so many times throughout my life, and that this help had come through that sacrament. Resisting the allure of the occult; not rising to the bait when teased by school friends about going to church; defending belief in God down the pub (never talk about politics and religion they say – especially when drinking!); not allowing myself to be taken down the rabbit hole of despair; standing up to the devil when tempted to resist reconciliation; hearing the gentle voice to come back to life. A good upbringing is one thing but, in spite of my seeming distance from God and the Church, and a fair amount of dissolute living, the Holy Spirit was always my helper and guide. I often think that things could have been a lot worse had I not already had the gift of the Holy Spirit within. This reminds me of Deuteronomy 32:11-12, which is prayed in Morning Prayer on Saturdays of Week 2 of the Psalter. My mum first pointed this out to me and said this was a word for me. God finds Israel in the desolate waste and surrounds him:

Like an eagle that watches over its nest,
that hovers over its young, so he spread his wings;
he took him, placed him on his outstretched wings.
The Lord alone was his guide
and no other God was with him.

ISAIAH 11: 1-2

The seven gifts of the Holy Spirit received at Confirmation equip us for our walk of discipleship. They are a sharing in the life of God. They are listed in Isaiah 11:1-2. Who could not be overawed with the thought that wisdom, understanding, right judgement, courage, knowledge, reverence and wonder are infused into us? They are given to us for our sanctification. This is what Jesus promised and this is what Jesus delivers when, with the Father, they pour the Holy Spirit out upon us. So much of what I recount in the earlier part of my journey is about these gifts really coming alive in me. They had been present and, as I mentioned above, had been helping me in unknown ways, but with the baptism in the Holy Spirit they truly came to the fore.

Courage was suddenly clear to me. There was a boldness in wanting to speak about Jesus. I was unafraid to share what was happening to me, even in environments which seemed to be mocking of faith, particularly the workplace. Wisdom, Understanding and Knowledge really came alive in me. It was like I was on a totally different plane. Right Judgement was apparent in the decisions I was taking. Reverence was awakened in me for the holy all around us, be it in the liturgy, or the majesty of God's creation in our fellow human beings. As for a deep sense of Wonder and Awe, particularly at the beauty of creation, well that really took off as I describe in chapter 19.

CHARISMATIC GIFTS OF THE HOLY SPIRIT
The gifts of the Holy Spirit described above, wonderful as they are, are not the only gifts the Holy Spirit bestows upon God's people. It is right to give a really good and solid catechesis regarding the seven gifts of the Holy Spirit to those preparing for Confirmation. These stand us in such good stead. They aid us in witnessing to Jesus. They are amazing, sanctifying gifts and we need to set them free if we haven't done so already. However, with the Holy Spirit there is so much more, and that needs to be explained to young and old.

There are other spiritual gifts, which are clearly described in the letters of St Paul, particularly 1 Corinthians 12: 7-11 (see beginning of chapter). These gifts are given as a grace at a particular time in order to help Jesus' followers in their walk of witness. There are gifts that are given to empower us as Jesus' disciples and to assist us in proclaiming Jesus and building up the Church. These gifts are dynamite. They are not explored enough, and yet they are there. We see them on display in the Acts of the Apostles and they are still there for us today. We can't witness to Christ in our own power. No, we have been given the Holy Spirit to assist us. There are those gifts of the Holy Spirit already within, as per Isaiah 11, and those which can come to us at the appropriate moment. The word 'gifts' in the context of St Paul's letters comes from the Greek 'charismata'. St. Paul describes these 'charismata' or charisms as 'manifestations' of the Holy Spirit.

Whilst I had experienced some of these charisms in 2000 after being baptised in the Holy Spirit, it was not until 2011 that I really came to understand them. It took eleven years, with no one in my priestly formation ever really talking about these charisms of the Holy Spirit, to come to a better understanding of what is on offer.

It is possible to subdivide these gifts into three areas. There are **gifts of power**, which really show forth the truth of the gospel in an incredible way. These would be healing and miracles and I look at these in the next chapter. There are also **gifts of prayer**, such as the gift of tongues, which aid in worshipping God and interceding on behalf of others. I discuss the gift of tongues in chapter 14. For the moment, we look at the **word gifts**, which assist us in the proclamation of the gospel and in leading people more deeply into the mystery of God's love.

PROPHECY

I love that prayer, often attributed to St Oscar Romero but actually written by Fr Ken Untener, where it says that we are 'prophets of a future not our own'. Prophecy is a hugely important gift to the church. We are reminded that through our baptism we are prophets. We share in Jesus' prophetic ministry as discussed in the previous chapter. We are people who speak truth and are able to share something of God's will through the supernatural gift of prophecy. It is really special when people are open to this charism in our parishes as it helps to build vision and faith. Prophecy is a manifestation of the Holy Spirit. It can be given to anyone at any time. Some people may flourish more in their openness to this charism. With courage, though, I am sure there are plenty of prophetic words and images in our parishes to come from those who are not yet aware of this charism.

There was an example of prophecy in our parishes a couple of years ago. Caroline, who is our Parish Outreach Worker, had been experiencing some of the frustration that can go with parish life. A prayerful lady, I am sure she had taken these frustrations to the Lord. She woke up one morning with the words, 'They're doing it wrong' ringing in her ears. She then proceeded to write down a vision to seek to reform, renew and transform our parishes; to change the way we do things, which is so often focused on maintenance as opposed to mission. She shared it with me with some trepidation but I immediately knew it was of the Lord. It was steeped in Scripture; heartfelt, and offered in humility. The words were challenging, which is usually a good sign. We need to move out of our comfort zone and the Holy Spirit helps with that. I knew what she shared was dynamite.

I shared these prophetic words with several people. They gave me, as the Parish Priest, the confidence to move forward with a vision for two parishes to join with another two. We would come together as a 'Mission Area' under the banner of 'Called to More', which was actually the title of Caroline's prophetic utterance. It gave us the confidence to go to the diocese with this proposal because it was so obviously of the Lord. In reality, the prophetic vision was actually seeking something even bigger and wider than what we are doing now. Sometimes we have to move forward in smaller steps. However, the prophecy has given me the courage to seek to encourage others within our diocese to reconsider our structures for the sake of mission. This looks very promising. Prophecy is not about foretelling the future but giving courage to move forward into the future with hope and vision.

Prophecy doesn't just come in words. It can come through pictures. In 2014, I was invited to preach at a large gathering in Mbarara, in the south of Uganda. I imagine there were at least 10,000 people there that day. Prior to going to the event, three of us who had been asked to share our testimonies prayed together. As we did so, a picture came into my mind of water gushing forth, like a waterfall rushing over the people. I sensed this was the Holy Spirit saying something about what was going to happen later – the Holy Spirit blessing and gracing those coming together in Jesus' name.

As I was preaching, I shared this picture and explained what I believed it meant. Lo, and behold, no sooner had I said this than it started to pour with rain. It hadn't rained for a long time. It was the driest time of year. Those gathered started to really dance and rejoice. They needed the rain but they also recognised that this was a sign of God's blessing. The rain was so heavy we actually had to stop proceedings for an hour, but the people kept on dancing and singing. The presence of the Holy Spirit was tangible. The people were hailing me as a prophet. In reality, on that day I was. I had shared the prophetic image. Praise Jesus!

Whilst I have had other pictures from the Holy Spirit, which have also been prophetic in nature and have helped to shape vision for mission and ministry, this was one I knew had to be shared more widely. It's an example of a manifestation of the Holy Spirit. If I hadn't shared that image that day, the event would have simply been a wash out. Having shared it, the people made a much deeper connection to how much God loves them. I'm sure it was empowering them in their walk of discipleship; their appreciation of the love of Jesus. We need the gift of courage to share these prophetic words and pictures. We know who gives us the courage, too!

UTTERANCE OF WISDOM & KNOWLEDGE

St Paul speaks earlier in the First Letter to the Corinthians about how we have been enriched by the grace of Christ in every way including speech and knowledge. He goes on to talk about how the true wisdom of God is what believers share (1 Cor 12: 8). It happens that we can receive, from the Holy Spirit, words of knowledge and words of wisdom which can be spoken into the lives of others. For example, I have found myself praying with someone and a word has come into my mind about that person. This would be some knowledge of that person which I couldn't have known before. When these words of knowledge are shared, this can really build up the faith of both the person being prayed for and the one praying too. This can be a catalyst for healing as expectant faith is increased. These words come into the mind as a super-natural gift. We don't possess them. The Holy Spirit places them upon our hearts and minds and enables us to articulate them. They are manifestations of the Holy Spirit.

The charismatic gift of wisdom is different to the natural wisdom that comes with age. It is also different to the gift of wisdom witnessed to in Isaiah 11, which is sanctifying wisdom. In my experience there have been times that I have found myself speaking wise words, that I have never really thought about before, in a prayerful time with some-one. These are words which touch the other person, although I am thinking, 'Where did that come from?' Words of wisdom and knowledge often go together. What we are talking about here is a manifestation of the Holy Spirit at a particular time for the building up of the Body of Christ. This could occur in a large gathering or on a one-to-one as has often been my experience. The point is that the Holy Spirit wants to assist us more than we can know. We don't do it in our power.

FAITH
I talked about how I received the gift of faith in 2000 when I got on my knees and asked, 'Lord, show me what I should do with my life'. I know that in that instant I was given the charismatic gift of faith. I knew that what I was asking, God

would do for me. I had never experienced that before. The Holy Spirit gave me the gift of faith at that precise moment to believe that God would do for me what I was asking. As said previously, sharing words of knowledge and wisdom can help to build faith. They can open us to the supernatural gift of faith in a particular moment. Expectant faith is something we want to build up in ourselves and our parishes, but the charismatic gift of faith is a 'one-off' moment – something very beautiful; amazing!

EVANGELISTS & TEACHERS
Whilst the list of charismatic gifts in 1 Corinthians is most well-known, there are also further gifts talked about in Romans 12:6-9 and Ephesians 4:7-14. We hear especially about the gift of evangelists and teachers. I talk about evangelists in chapter 12. For the moment, though, it is essential to remember that all these gifts on offer are for the whole Body of Christ. They are there for all the People of God. These are not gifts solely for the clergy. Far from it! My experience is that the lay faithful really flourish in their openness to the charismatic gifts more than the clergy do. We are all in this together. The clergy do have a responsibility to assist in the discernment of charisms.

DISCERNMENT
I want to give a final word here to the gift of discernment, which is also recognised as a charism of the Holy Spirit. Discernment of spirits is really important. We know that the Holy Spirit blows where the Holy Spirit chooses (John 3:8).

We also know that the Holy Spirit is the soul of the Church and not only brings unity but is unity. The Holy Spirit is there to guard that unity; to guard the People of God from the evil one. Discernment is crucial in this regard.

I remember going for my interview for being accepted as a candidate for Ordination to the Diaconate, a year prior to the Ordination to Priesthood. As I had been in a previous seminary, one of the priest staff members didn't know me that well. I felt I got a real grilling. It knocked me sideways. Sensing later that I was somewhat shocked, he said to me, 'We had to be morally certain it was right'. Years later, I get his point. Discernment is really important. I had clearly discerned that I was called to Priesthood but the Church needed to confirm this.

When I was first ordained I wanted to rush at everything. There were times when I thought the Holy Spirit had inspired an idea, which seemed so obvious, only to realise that it wasn't a good idea. It's not that the devil is always directly at work but sometimes our own pride can get in the way. Yes, the Holy Spirit can surely work in spite of that but care does need to be taken at times over decisions. Prayerful discernment is essential. This doesn't mean going slow on everything. It means testing the spirits. God, Satan, the world, the flesh. We need to take this to prayer and listen. Sharing ideas with other prayerful people is useful. Again, listening carefully; looking for light. It really is a case of asking the Holy Spirit for the inspiration.

FOR REFLECTION & DISCUSSION

Reflect on the gifts of the Holy Spirit as listed in Isaiah 11:1-2

How have you seen these gifts active in your life? Do you want to see them more prevalent?

Reflect on the charismatic gifts of the Holy Spirit as described above. Share your experiences of these?

Do you want to see more of this Holy Spirit action in your life.

Do you see how we are called to greater things?

How are you getting along so far with this book?

Song: *Street Called Mercy* by Hillsong United

10

Healing in
the Spirit

'Very truly, I tell you, the one who believes in me
will also do the works that I do and, in fact,
will do greater works than these,
because I am going to the Father.'
John 14:12

WITNESS BOOTS

'Will you be at the event at the cathedral this afternoon?'
asked my friend, Una, a parishioner of St Peter's,
Gloucester, the first parish that I served in. 'I've got
something to tell you'.

'Yes, I will be', I replied. 'Let's have a catch up. I'll see you
by the Blessed Sacrament chapel'.

Una, a great spiritual support, was in her sixties. She had
problems with her feet that had gradually got worse as she
had got older. They were both misshapen and neither of
them could flex. There was no feeling in them at all. She
had been told by medical experts that they would never
get better. Her right ankle didn't articulate normally. On
both of her feet she wore special orthopaedic shoes. She
walked with the aid of a stick. She struggled terribly with
steps. But there she was on that afternoon at Clifton

cathedral, standing upright, no stick in sight, wearing a pair of bright, colourful Dr Marten boots with flowers on them. 'These are my witness boots', she proclaimed. 'I've had an incredible healing'.

She proceeded to tell me that a few weeks earlier she had been to a prayer group meeting where 'prayer ministry' was being offered. There were two ladies praying with her, both also from the parish of St Peter's. As they prayed with her, focusing particularly on her feet and ankles, one of them was given a picture in her mind's eye. It was of Jesus pouring his Precious Blood over Una's feet. As she spoke this vision aloud, Una says she could suddenly feel her feet. This was the first healing.

Not long after, she went to a Celebrate Weekend in Bristol and when the speaker asked if anyone wanted to witness to healing, she decided to go forward to the stage. As she did so, she felt like she was stuck to the spot and she felt bones moving in her feet and ankles. An incredible healing had taken place and her friend, who had prayed with her previously, again told her that she had seen the same picture of Jesus pouring his Precious Blood over her feet.

Finally, when Una went to see her doctor, he could not explain what had happened. As a man of faith, he could only give praise to God and acknowledge that a miraculous healing had taken place. Una said to him there was still a little bit more work to be done on the feet and that he should pray with her. He did so. He took her feet and prayed and there was more movement of bones and the healing was perfected.

'That's not what I expected first thing on a Monday morning', he exclaimed!

JESUS THE HEALER
What had happened to Una? How did this all come about? Well, the Holy Spirit had given a special charism of healing to the two prayer ministers and her doctor, as discussed in the previous chapter. This charism is not something that was within the three of them. It was a supernatural gift given at that particular moment (see 2 Cor 12:9). Some people clearly have an openness to this charism but it is generally not a gift that they actually possess. As for Una, she was almost certainly open to the possibility of healing. She had faith. Jesus healed when he recognised faith (see Luke 5:20). St Paul, empowered by the Holy Spirit, did the same when he recognised faith (see Acts 14:8-14).

Jesus healed during his earthly ministry. There were lots of physical healings. Jesus promised that what he did on earth would continue after his Ascension. So, after Pentecost we see lots of healings in the Acts of the Apostles. Such events are signs of the Kingdom of God in our midst. They are God's sovereign work, the action of the Holy Spirit, and they will still happen today if only we would be open to the possibility and have faith. In Una's case, as with many physical healings, the healing is there to be witnessed to, to be shared, in order to build up the faith of others. The Holy Spirit heals so that the one healed and those who see what has happened are able to say 'Jesus is Lord' with ever greater fervour. Healing and mission are inextricably linked.

TIP OF THE ICEBERG

What I have described is only the tip of the iceberg. There is so much healing that takes place both inside and outside of the Church. As I was writing this, Una wanted to remind me how she has received many other less dramatic healings simply through prayerful connectedness to God. On one occasion when this happened, she received these words from Psalm 127:2

> In vain is your earlier rising your going later to rest, you who toil for the bread you eat: when he pours gifts on his beloved while they slumber.

I, too, know that I have received and continue to receive a great deal of healing. One occasion that sticks in my mind was back in 2000, shortly after being baptised in the Holy Spirit. It was only a few weeks after so many Spirit-filled moments had touched and utterly changed my life but somehow I felt a depression coming over me. It seemed to weigh heavy on my head. There was a huge positivity within me but something didn't feel right. I had previously given up smoking various substances and wondered whether there was even some withdrawal. I prayed that this might be lifted from me. Shortly after this I felt something in my head, like a little 'pump' starting up. This 'pump' squirted something over my brain – I know it sounds mad. I could actually feel the liquid being squirted and the sensation of it over the top of my brain. Suffice to say that what was hanging over me just dissipated. Alleluia!

PRAYER MINISTRY

Since 2011, when I went to the Life in the Spirit Seminars and came to understand baptism in the Holy Spirit, I have seen a lot of healing take place especially when people have been open to what the Holy Spirit wants to do. This has been particularly notable at gatherings organised by Catholic Charismatic Renewal (CCR), such as Celebrate, New Dawn or diocesan CCR events. This has normally been within the context of well-organised and well-trained 'prayer ministry' teams.

These 'prayer ministry' teams pray with individuals. They open themselves to any promptings of the Holy Spirit and share these. Often what God reveals to them brings an increase in faith in both the person being prayed for and the praying teams themselves. When this happens, the possibility of healing really grows as does the likelihood of baptism in the Holy Spirit. It is also important to mention the work of the Cor et Lumen Christi community, who devote themselves to this kind of work, witnessing to the Risen Jesus and ramping up the work of the Holy Spirit through their 'Healing and Miracles' rallies, which truly serve as a witness to the healing work of the Blessed Trinity.

In our parishes, I have tried to kickstart 'prayer ministry' after Mass, where we invite people with particular ailments or spiritual concerns to come forward to be prayed with. There often seems to be a reticence to people approaching this, although there have been experiences of healing through this ministry. It is also difficult to find people confident enough to step up to participate as ministers and engage in training for this beautiful work of love. This is why baptism in the Holy Spirit is so important. Fanning into a flame the gifts that have been given to us and coming alive in Jesus and the Holy Spirit is what is needed. Yes, we need to keep putting it out there that Jesus heals. Jesus and the Father pour the Holy Spirit out and bring healing. The root of the word 'salvation' comes from 'healing'.

SACRAMENT OF THE SICK

Through my priestly ministry, I have come to an ever-deepening awareness of the importance of the Sacrament of the Sick with regard to healing. We can never discount the possibility of physical healing with this Sacrament, however, my experience has often been of profound spiritual healing. There have been many times when a final anointing has clearly lifted a burden from a dying person, who has then gone on to die in peace. I have had families recount how they could visibly see the change in a loved one after an anointing with the Oil of the Sick. The sacrament has all the hallmarks of the Holy Spirit about it. A laying on of hands; anointing with oil on the forehead and hands and this beautiful prayer to accompany it. This is a Spirit-filled encounter with Jesus.

Through this holy anointing, may the Lord in his love
and mercy help you with the grace of the Holy Spirit.
May the Lord who frees you from sin save you and
raise you up.

Early in my priestly ministry there was a particular incident
where God wanted to show me how important this
sacrament is. I know the Holy Spirit wanted me to share this.

GO BACK!

I had been asked to visit a lady who was dying with just a
couple of weeks to live. Her husband told me she hadn't
been near the parish church for twenty-five years or more
but she wanted a priest to visit. It was Holy Thursday and
a lot was going on in preparation for the Easter festivities
and my head was a bit scrambled. I arrived at the house,
a ten-minute drive from the presbytery, and as I got out of
the car I realised that I had left the Holy Oil behind. I
thought to myself that there was no point going back but
decided to visit the lady, give her a blessing, and then go
back in Easter Week to anoint her as I'd been told she was
expected to live for another couple of weeks. As I turned
from the car to go to the house, I couldn't move. I was
rooted to the spot and a voice said in my mind, 'Go,
back!' It was a clear command from the Holy Spirit. I had
to go back to the presbytery and get the oil and then
come back again. So that's what I did.

On Easter Sunday afternoon, Fr Liam told me that the husband had phoned and said that his wife had died peacefully that morning. He wanted to thank me for having anointed her because it brought her great peace. This to me was evidence of how important this sacrament is. The Holy Spirit made it clear. The effect of this sacrament is a gift of the Holy Spirit, uniting us more closely to the Crucified and Risen Christ. It is a sharing in Jesus' saving work, bringing healing and preparation for the journey through death to eternal life.

SO MUCH MORE TO SAY

What I offer in this chapter is so ridiculously tiny. Imagine the thousands of books written on this subject. I simply want us to be reminded that, among the many ways that healing comes to us, physical healing is very real and possible. Physical healing occurs to help build the faith of others and witness to Jesus Christ. Let us build our faith and expectation for this. Also, prayer ministry, where we train people to pray with others is an extension of our welcome and loving concern for the People of God. With the Holy Spirit more active in our parishes in this way, it will be a great way of evangelising. Finally, the Sacrament of the Sick is a powerful encounter with Christ in the power of the Holy Spirit and draws us to the heart of the Father.

So, when it comes to healing, remember Jesus' command to 'Heal the sick' (Matthew 10:8) and, of course, don't forget the Holy Spirit.

FOR REFLECTION & DISCUSSION

What is your reaction to Una's healing as described above? Why do you think it happened? What was the purpose of it?

Which are your favourite healing stories in the Gospel. Can you list them down and share them?

Can you share your own experiences of healing?

Do you see the value of regular prayer for healing before offered in our parishes? Are you prepared to make it happen?

Song: *Awake My Soul* **by Hillsong Worship**

11

Sin and Reconciliation

'...he breathed on them and said to them,
'Receive the Holy Spirit'. If you forgive
the sins of any, they are forgiven them;
if you retain the sins of any, they are retained.'
(John 20:22-23)

THE FORGIVENESS OF SINS

Christ speaks to us through St Paul in Romans 5:5 when we are told that, 'Hope does not disappoint us, because God's love has been poured into our hearts through the Holy Spirit that has been given to us.' The Father and the Son pour out the Holy Spirit, who is love. The first gift of this love is the forgiveness of sins just as we see when Jesus appears to the disciples after the resurrection. He breathes on them as a sign and foretaste of the fullness of the Holy Spirit to come at Pentecost. He tells them that forgiveness of sins is the priority of this new and intense experience of the dynamic love of the Blessed Trinity.

In my personal reflections regarding the early part of my journey, I am aware that it is always the Holy Spirit who took the initiative. The Holy Spirit prompted, led and guided. The Holy Spirit is the one who wanted me to know and proclaim Jesus as Lord and to know the Father's heart. It was the Holy Spirit who led me to seek forgiveness as the gateway and preparation for the coming revelation. The forgiveness of sins was crucial. Being reconciled to God and the Church was an essential precursor to the baptism in the Holy Spirit. That is why the Holy Spirit jumped in so forcefully and made me speak the words, 'Get behind me Satan' when I considered not going to the Sacrament at the beginning of 2000. Forgiveness. Reconciliation. There is such beauty and majesty in God's sovereign work.

We know that baptism is the first sacrament for the forgiveness of sins, which erases the effects of original sin within us. This is the washing of regeneration of the Holy Spirit. The action of the Holy Spirit in this sacrament, in making us new creations in Christ, is so apparent in the symbols used of water, oil, light, and being clothed. Post baptism, we know that we can be open to God's forgiveness in many ways. It is the Sacrament of Reconciliation, though, which is the surest path for us to be fully reconciled to God and our fellow brothers and sisters. The Holy Spirit brings us face to face with Jesus, who looks tenderly upon us and, with the Father, both breathe out forgiveness; true healing for the soul.

THINKING ABOUT SIN
There is a beautiful litany of the Holy Spirit which I have prayed before in the church, which asks for so many great graces. One of the lines of the litany is, 'Holy Spirit, inspire us with horror of sin'. I have often found that a challenging line. The word 'horror' is one that hasn't sat

comfortably with me. It has jarred in some way. The image that comes to mind is of Edvard Munch's, 'The Scream' – that harrowing picture of terror and pure panic. However, on reflection, this is an appropriate reaction. Horror is defined as an intense feeling of fear, shock, or disgust. If sin can have absolutely no part in God; if sin is a turning away from God, who is love, then surely it should inspire a strong reaction. How often do we really feel that way? We forget about sin at our own peril.

We often talk about a loss of a sense of sin within society and, naturally, this has an effect amongst the People of God. If we see ourselves without sin then we are kidding ourselves, and it becomes difficult to allow the power of Christ to reign over our hearts. We need to reimagine sin and allow the Holy Spirit to give us a new understanding. I don't have the magic bullet here but offer some brief points below.

POURED OUT

As a priest, I hear a lot of Confessions. I wish I heard more. Celebrating the Sacrament of Reconciliation is a great joy because it is at the heart of my priestly calling. Standing at the altar and offering the eternal sacrifice of praise and sitting with someone who is seeking God's forgiveness. These are the two places where my ministry makes most sense. I have seen how this sacrament has brought great healing. I have heard people describe how they have felt significantly lighter after the celebration. I know lives that have been turned around through the liberation of God's love in this sacrament. I have experienced it myself after all. This is the ultimate preparation for baptism in the Holy Spirit.

I love the Prayer of Absolution. The Trinitarian nature of it is so powerful. It is a simple explanation of what we believe. God has reconciled the world to himself through the death and resurrection of Jesus Christ, and the Holy Spirit has been sent to bring forgiveness.

> God, the Father of mercies,
> through the death and resurrection of his Son
> has reconciled the world to himself
> and sent the Holy Spirit among us
> for the forgiveness of sins;
> through the ministry of the Church
> may God grant you pardon and peace,
> and I absolve you from your sins
> in the name of the Father, and of the Son,
> and of the Holy Spirit.

The word 'sent' in this prayer is very powerful. It is as if the Holy Spirit has a mission – to bring about the forgiveness of sins. The Father and the Son send their mutual love, which is mysteriously inseparable from them, upon us. The word 'sent' in this prayer is being changed in the English translation to 'poured out'. Reflecting on this, I really love that image. I have always imagined the Holy Spirit being 'poured out' constantly like an endless jug of water tipped up and splashing over us. It ties in with the quote from Romans 5:5 above. Forgiveness is lavishly poured upon us.

EXAMINATION OF CONSCIENCE

Over the years I have come to realise that I need the Holy Spirit to really point out to me the more subtle areas of my sinfulness. Some things are obvious but others less so. We need light to be shed on all areas of our lives. The more we are honest with ourselves and God, the more clearly we can hear God's voice. It's like tuning in to a station on an old radio. We need to get rid of the static in order to get a crisp reception.

The Holy Spirit assists us when we reflect on our lives and ask how they accord with the values of Jesus. The Ten Commandments offer a sure basis to examine our conscience. The Beatitudes can help us tap deeper into the heart of Christ. We could consider less of 'what are the things that we've done', but rather 'what are the things we have failed to do'. In this day and age, we would do well to reflect on our relationship with creation and how we are shaping up in our ecological choices. In the end, this is not about beating ourselves up but being really honest before God to give space for the soul to expand.

If you are seeking to open yourself to baptism in the Holy Spirit then take heart. Allow the Holy Spirit to show you where forgiveness is needed. Ask the Holy Spirit to show you where you are not living like Jesus. Seek the guidance of a good Christian guide. Build up a desire for repentance and then open yourself to celebrating the Sacrament of Reconciliation. Be assured of a great welcome. Do not be afraid!

FOR REFLECTION & DISCUSSION

'If we see ourselves without sin then we are kidding ourselves, and it becomes difficult to allow the power of Christ to reign over our hearts.'
Discuss

How seriously do you take sin?

Reflect on the Prayer of Absolution

Do you recognise the beauty of the gift of the Sacrament of Reconciliation?

Do you ask the Holy Spirit to help you make a good examination of conscience?

Are you excited about wanting more of the gifts of the Holy Spirit?

Shout aloud, 'Jesus is Lord' and then keep that mantra going in your mind.

Song: *You Were On The Cross* by Matt Maher

12

Preaching
in the Spirit

*'If I proclaim the gospel, this gives me
no grounds for boasting, for an obligation
is laid on me, and woe to me
if I do not proclaim the gospel!'*
1 Corinthians 9:16

HERALDS
'I don't know how you do it, Father Matt. How do you just stand up and preach without notes and somehow it all makes sense?' That has been asked of me on many an occasion.

The answer to this question is always to remind people that I'm not 'winging it'. There is a lot of preparation that goes into this. There is also an essential reliance on Jesus and the power of the Holy Spirit.

From the earliest days of my calling to the priesthood, there has been this sense within me that I was called to be a preacher. Of course, preaching is linked to ordination but this felt like it was something more than that. I spent five years with the Redemptorists, who are a preaching congregation, and imagined myself preaching missions. Ultimately, though, this was not God's plan for me.

Whilst at St John's Seminary in Wonersh, I remember a class with the Rector, in which he was talking about 'models of priesthood'. By this, I don't mean priests on a catwalk! We were discussing which aspects of priesthood we felt our gifts were ordered to. For me, I felt strongly about a 'herald model'. That is to say, exercising priestly ministry in its full but having an awareness of the centrality of and desire for proclamation of the Gospel. It's not lost on me now that the first homily I preached as a deacon was on the Solemnity of St Peter and St Paul. It was focused on the need for renewed missionary vigour and vitality in our parishes, modelling ourselves on these two heroes of our faith.

STEPPING OUT

I have always enjoyed preaching.   I consider it an incredible privilege and believe, based on the testimony of others, that I have been given a gift in this area. I have seen my preaching develop over time. For the first couple of years after ordination, I would always write my homilies. I would give the appropriate care and attention to prep-aration and then seek to write them in such a way as it wasn't obvious that it was written. I felt, though, that there was a need to step away from the text, but I didn't feel confident to do that. That all changed after my experience of the Life in the Spirit Seminars in 2011.

I had always been impressed by preachers who were obviously not reading their homilies. I'm not saying this is a better way of preaching but something had spoken to me about this style of preaching. I was always very taken with the preaching style of Fr Liam when I was at St Mary's, Swindon and when I was his assistant priest at St Peter's, Gloucester. It was as though he was preaching from the heart in a very natural but Spirit-filled way. That, for me, was the difference – the Holy Spirit.

The Life in the Spirit Seminars helped me to reassess my preaching and I found a new confidence with the Holy Spirit. I went on a charismatic priests' retreat and there the retreat giver gave some advice which has remained with me. She encouraged priests to do the necessary prayerful preparation for preaching. Then, when it comes to the preaching itself, she said, say a prayer to the Holy Spirit and step out in the power of the Risen Lord. That was dynamite. It was confirmed by someone else whom I had met, too, and with whom I had discussed my reticence to drop the text. Now, when I go to preach, I spend the time prayerfully with the Scripture, seek the inspiration of the Holy Spirit and mentally go through my homily. This probably takes longer than actually writing a homily. Then, when I come to preach, I say in my mind something like:

> Holy Spirit come to my aid now as I come to proclaim the Word. Help me to step out in the power of the Risen Christ.

The difference this made to my preaching was significant. This was attested to immediately by parishioners who commented how they felt the power of the proclamation, and hence the presence of the Holy Spirit, was heightened by doing this.

LAY EVANGELISTS
Let's make this clear – preaching isn't solely for those who are ordained. Yes, within the liturgy, especially the Mass, the Church is clear that this is a role reserved for those in Sacred Orders. However, the gift of evangelism is given by the Holy Spirit to plenty of people who are not ordained. Personally, I have been most impressed and moved by the preaching of lay evangelists. Hearing married or single men and women, old and young, witness to the power of Christ in their lives is an inspiration. Their gift is clear and their right to exercise their ministry is not to be restricted but encouraged. They have received their gift from the Holy Spirit and so they have a duty to use it. This is enshrined in the documents of the Second Vatican Council. We must allow this to flourish.

IT'S THE SPIRIT'S WORK
'Every time you go out to preach, it knocks an hour off your life', said one of my brother diocesan priests as we were reflecting on this subject. I think he was alluding to a certain sense of trepidation which comes with the preaching ministry. This is God's Word and it's all too easy to be flippant about it, or get in the way of it. What amazes me about preaching, though, is that the Holy Spirit communicates to the listener what the Holy Spirit wants to communicate in spite of us. There have been many times that someone has said to me, 'I love what you said about

such and such'. I'm often there thinking to myself, 'I'm certain I never said that at all'. Also, it's usually the homilies I'm less sure of that get the most positive comments. When I think I've 'knocked it out of the park' it is usually when there's no affirmation at all, for pride has got in the way. That's the beauty of the Holy Spirit.

If you're called to break open the Word and preach, take heart! All Scripture is Christ. The Word of God is utterly alive and active. Have great reverence for it. Keep close to Jesus. Allow the Holy Spirit to stir your heart and mind. Pray. Prepare. Then step out with the aid of the Holy Spirit and in the power of the Risen Jesus. Don't forget the Holy Spirit is with you.

FOR REFLECTION & DISCUSSION

Work on your testimony. What would you want to share with others about your journey with Jesus and your experience of the Holy Spirit?

Are you ready to give your testimony? Can you trust that the Risen Lord is with you; the Holy Spirit is upholding you; guiding you?

Song: *Shout to the North* by Delirious

13

Joy -
A Beautiful Fruit

'You will draw water joyfully
from the wellsprings of salvation.'
Isaiah 12:3

THE FRUITS OF THE HOLY SPIRIT

'What are your favourite fruits?' I asked the Year 2 class of 6-year-olds. We were going to be talking about the fruits of the Holy Spirit. 'Banana' said one, 'Apple' said another and so on. Then one little boy piped up, 'My favourite fruit is a cantaloupe'. I was rather taken aback and tickled by the sophistication of the young man. I hadn't expected that! There are many fruits to be had. I was recently in Egypt on holiday with my sister and revelled in the fresh figs, dates and, wait for it young man – kumquats. Beat that!

In the letter to the Galatians (5:22-23), St Paul speaks of the variety of special fruits that those who walk in the Holy Spirit should expect to see. To be associated with Christ; to be in Him; these are the fruits, allowed to grow and mature by the Holy Spirit that should set us apart from non-believers. He says that 'the fruit of the Spirit is love, joy, peace, patience, kindness, generosity, faithfulness, gentleness and self-control'. Each of these fruits deserves not just a chapter but several books. Let's face it, 'God is love' (1 John 4:8), and 'God so loved the world...' (John 3:16). Simply to reflect on love, the very being of God, the gift given, the fruit experienced, would fill all the books in the world. I want here simply to reflect on my experience of one particular fruit of the Holy Spirit – joy.

FLEETING JOY

I was recently watching my niece's husband playing with their 18-month-old son, Finley. Daddy was lying on his back and holding his baby boy up and then pulling him in close and blowing 'raspberries' on his neck. Finley's laughter and his obvious delight in this moment of fun and tenderness was an outpouring of joy. It was wonderful to watch. Joy seems to be pure in children, perhaps untainted by the weariness and cynicism of the world which can come with age.

Sometimes we can see mass experiences of joy. Recently Argentina won the football World Cup. What outpourings of joy there were in Buenos Aires and throughout that country. 'Hail the Messiah' was one headline in a newspaper, likening their golden boy, Lionel Messi, to Christ in an obvious play on his surname, as he brought temporary light relief and a diversion from their economic woes.

INFECTIOUS JOY

Joy as described above is only temporary. It is a fleeting experience. It can help to build us up from children to adults, but it is not the experience of joy that is on offer from Jesus Christ in the Holy Spirit. That joy is a lasting joy. It is a joy that can be fed upon. Perhaps more correctly, it is a joy that we can drink from, just as Jesus describes to the Samaritan woman at the well (John 4:10-14). This is the water of the Holy Spirit that will never run out. Never will we be thirsty with this water. The joy that comes with this water of the Holy Spirit is constantly accessible within. This does not mean constant laughter or dancing and praising aloud. This is not a fleeting joy but a reality of God within us and the Holy Spirit having been fully unbound within us. It is the beauty of joy which brings us strength in good times and bad; in consolation or desolation; in fulness of health or sickness. It is a joy that radiates. A joy that flows out to others.

For me, at first, this experience of joy was intoxicating. Perhaps it was because I had experienced the polar opposite for such a long time and now everything had changed in the blink of an eye. I felt so alive, so much welling up inside and flooding my senses. So intoxicating was this joy that I almost crashed my car coming home from work one evening. I had a nice little company sports car. My boss always said that it cornered on rails. Flooded with joy that evening and feeling invincible (note the pride coming in!), I went too quickly into a large roundabout with a camber on it and span the vehicle. Somehow I missed the oncoming traffic by going side on into a traffic island on the other side of the roundabout. Suffice to say that I wasn't allowing the fruit of self-control to get in. At least there isn't a police breathalyser for joy for I was over the limit that night. I did need a new rear axle though.

Certainly joy was very apparent to me over that first year or more. Regardless of this, joy wasn't something I ever really thought about until after the Life in the Spirit Seminars in 2011. It was from here that I had a deepened aware-ness of the language and experience of the Holy Spirit. It was around this time that I really had settled into the practice of celebrating Mass as a new priest. Parishioners started commenting on the joy that I seemed to bring and show through the exercise of my priesthood, especially when preaching and standing at the altar. I was regularly told that I was the 'smiling priest'. I'm pretty sure it wasn't that I had an inane grin on my face, but apparently my faced showed something of what was going on inside me.

KEEP GETTING TOPPED UP

There are times that I have felt joy wane in my life and my ministry. These have usually been periods where my trust and faithfulness to prayer have slipped. There are times in our lives when anxiety and pressure might creep in. It is on some of these occasions that I have not always been quick enough to call on the Holy Spirit. The frustration of parish life and its challenges has, on occasion, swamped me. It is when this happens that I really need to stay close to Jesus and ask the Holy Spirit to fan into a flame the gifts and let the fruits come forth.

JOY IN OUR PARISHES

I see a lot of joyful people in our parishes. There are many parishioners who, perhaps unaware to themselves, demonstrate that beautiful fruit of the Holy Spirit. They are very inspiring. On the other hand, there is a great deal of a lack of joy in many parishioners. Faith still keeps them close to Christ and the Church but somehow something is missing. The fruits of the Holy Spirit, particularly joy, don't seem to be apparent. That is why baptism in the Holy Spirit makes such a difference. There is a flatness in many of our parishes, and the gifts and subsequent fruits of the Holy Spirit need to be set free. Joy can and must be the mark of our parish life and witness.

Pope Francis speaks of contagious joy being the catalyst for mission in and through our parishes. His first encyclical was, of course, entitled 'The Joy of the Gospel'. He opens with the line, 'The joy of the Gospel fills the hearts and lives of all who encounter Jesus'. He also treats of joy in his Apostolic Exhortation, 'Rejoice and Be Glad'. Here he talks about the Christian life being 'joy in the Holy Spirit' as he picks up on St Paul's words to the Romans (14:17).

> 'For the kingdom of God is not food and drink but righteousness and peace and joy in the Holy Spirit.'

FOR REFLECTION & DISCUSSION

'The fruit of the Spirit is love, joy, peace, patience, kindness, generosity, faithfulness, gentleness and self-control'. Gal 5:22-23

Spend a good time with this word and then reflect on where you see these fruits in your life. List each one and find an example for each one.

Where do you find joy in your life? Do you sense it welling up in you? If not, can you name why and perhaps seek prayer for this?

'The joy of the Lord is your strength' (Nehemiah 8:10) Discuss

Keep invoking the Holy Spirit and praising the name of Jesus.

Song: *Joy* by Rend Collective

14

A Taste
for Praise

'Praise the Lord!
Praise the Lord, O my soul!
I will praise the Lord as long as I live;
I will sing praises to my God all my life long.'
Psalm 146 1:2

O PRAISE THE LORD, ALL YOU NATIONS

One of the effects of baptism in the Holy Spirit that I have become more and more conscious of over the years, particularly after the events of 2011, is a taste for praise. I find myself deep within and consciously in my mind just saying, 'Praise you Jesus'. It's like a mantra going round and round. Whether I'm waiting in a queue at the supermarket, riding up a long Mendip hill, writing a book:

'Praise you Jesus. Praise you Jesus. Praise you Jesus'.

I think it's an answer to a prayer. It's certainly a super-natural gift.

On occasion I praise God with the gift of tongues, which most definitely is a supernatural gift of the Holy Spirit (see chapter 9). For me, personally, this is something that I feel is most suited to a worship gathering, when I am praising

God with others. Praying and praising in tongues with a group of worshippers can lead to a wonderful sound and bring about a fantastically positive Spirit-filled atmosphere. There are times, though, when I may praise God in tongues alone. It's not unknown in the shower! The words that come from my mouth are also a mantra. They are not words I could write down. There are just three of them which are uttered round and round. I sense they are simply words praising Father, Son and Holy Spirit.

The gift of praying in tongues is very beautiful and well worth exploring as a charism of the Holy Spirit. In my experience it is a gift which helps to open us up to the other charismatic gifts of the Holy Spirit, such as words of knowledge and wisdom, healing and prophecy. I have also found myself interceding in a 'warrior' style of tongue when praying with someone with some kind of demonic oppression or affliction. Don't resist this gift if you feel it coming to you.

ACCLAIM HIM ALL YOU PEOPLES

Praise music. I love praise music.

There are lots of different ways to praise God. There are lots of different styles of praise music. In most of our parishes we tend to use the more traditional hymns of which there are many fine old and new hymns of praise. I always encourage our musicians to consider using a rousing hymn of praise at the beginning of Mass in order to lift the People of God up as we begin the celebration of Sunday, the day of Resurrection. The liturgy is shot through with the Holy Spirit so we need to help our brothers and sisters to be lifted up by that same Spirit. It is good for people to be sent out with a hearty hymn of praise too. Celebration. Celebration. This is Good News after all.

When I say I love praise music, though, I'm really talking here about lively Spirit-filled worship music. It's not something we hear much of in our parishes as it's often difficult to find the musicians. When we have offered this style of worship music in our churches, the reaction has been overwhelmingly positive. I've sometimes wondered what the older parishioners might think, but I've been surprised by their openness to this. When are we having that again they will ask?

I only came to be aware of this kind of worship music through the Life in the Spirit Seminars and the subsequent involvement with prayer groups and Catholic Charismatic Renewal. I found the music infectious. Some parishioners at St Peter's in Gloucester made me my first 'mix-CD' and I haven't looked back. Ever since, unless I am listening to the radio, this is the only kind of music I play in the car. It enlivens me. It inspires me. I sing along and really know that I am praising God. The way the song writers have engaged with the Word of God makes the music alive, and I really feel the Holy Spirit communicating the love of Jesus to me. It moves me to tears at times. I love to share new songs with friends.

Parishioners in our four churches know about my love of worship music. I occasionally refer to songs in homilies as the words are generally very kerygmatic. They proclaim the basic truth which we are called to preach continually; the essence of the Gospel. God's love; salvation in Christ through faith; the Holy Spirit present amongst us. As I am writing this, a song that has been on my heart for the past few weeks has to be shared. These are the kind of lyrics which inspire me and move me. This is my story. This is your story.

The song is *God With Us* by Jesus Culture from the album *Let it Echo*. Just go online and search for it!

You are matchless in grace and mercy
There is nowhere we can hide from Your love
You are steadfast, never failing, You are faithful
All creation is in awe of who You are

You're the healer of the sick and the broken
You are comfort for every heart that mourns
Our King and our Saviour forever
For eternity we will sing of all You've done

We sing
God with us, God for us
Nothing could come against, no one can stand between us
God with us, God for us
Nothing could come against, no one can stand between us

Your heart, it moves with compassion
There is life, there is healing in Your love

You're the Father, the Son, the Holy Spirit
For eternity we will sing of all You've done

Where there was death, You brought life, Lord
Where there was fear, You brought courage
When I was afraid, You were with me
And You're lifting me up, and You're lifting me up

Everyone is different when it comes to musical choices. We all praise in different ways. Let's thank the Holy Spirit for our unity in diversity. Let's invoke the Holy Spirit to build up praise in us even more.

FOR REFLECTION & DISCUSSION

How do you like to praise God? Can you see how praise can open us more to the Holy Spirit's power?

Spend time with the image of Jesus praising and thanking his Father in Luke 10:21-23 or Matthew 11: 25-28

Write your own short praise song to glorify God.

What is the Holy Spirit doing in you now?

Song: *Never Gonna Stop Singing*
by Jesus Culture, featuring Kim Walker-Smith

15

Perseverance

'My brothers and sisters, whenever you face trials
of any kind, consider it nothing but joy,
because you know that the testing of your faith
produces endurance; and let endurance have
its full effect, so you may be mature
and complete, lacking in nothing.'
James 1:2-4

ENDURANCE

'How are you getting on in the seminary?' asked the elderly priest who had arrived to celebrate Sunday Mass at St John the Baptist, Trowbridge. I was staying in the parish for the summer to keep an eye on the place whilst the parish priest was away. 'Oh, you know. It's a bit of a drag', I said, rolling my eyes and perhaps looking for a bit of sympathy.

'Your job is to persevere!' he retorted. The comment rocked me back on my heals. 'Your job is to persevere.' Those words have rung in my ears ever since. The scenario brings a little wry smile to my face. These were words of encouragement in the form of a mild rebuke. The question, I ask, though, 'Is it really my job to persevere?'

Over the past twenty years, I have taken part in a lot of endurance activities. I have run full marathons for charity, and lots of half marathons in preparation. My knees are a bit dodgy now and so a few years ago I took up cycling. Combining a passion for Jesus, mission and promoting vocations, I cycled to every parish of Clifton Diocese over three weeks back in 2015. The next year, I cycled from Lands End to John O'Groats in nine days back-to-back, covering 970 miles. In 2018, still promoting vocations, I travelled to the Alps and the Pyrenees to cycle up some of the iconic climbs of the Tour de France. Such events require training and discipline. They also require fuelling the body correctly. We need to fuel our bodies correctly if we are going to endure. Without this we just can't carry on.

In the early days of going out on long bike rides, I have made the mistake of not taking enough fuel along. I have run out of energy bars and have ridden myself to a stand-still, ending up a shaking wreck. On one occasion I even had to call a taxi to get me back home because I had gone past the point of no return with regard to energy. As I've got more experienced this generally never happens, although there have been a couple of occasions more recently where I have been complacent. 'Oh, I'll be fine. I'll extend that 60-mile ride to 100. It doesn't matter if I haven't got any more food on me and there are no shops around'. Always a mistake. There is a need to remain sharp at all times.

EYES ON JESUS

When it comes to discipleship, we are called to keep our eyes on Jesus. We know that he is with us always, just as he said he would be. That presence is communicated to us by the Holy Spirit. That same Holy Spirit strengthen us and graces us with the ability to endure. There is an act of will on our part. We need to keep saying 'yes' to Jesus. We have to be careful not to get complacent. We need to invoke the Holy Spirit, but the act of perseverance isn't something that we do in our own strength.

I am 52 years old and am coming up to thirteen years of ordination as a priest. There are times when I wonder how I've lasted this long. When I go to jubilee celebrations of priests who have been ordained for 25, 40, 50 or 60 years, I ask the same question. How have they lasted so long? The answer is simple, though. As long as we are faithful and seek the Lord as best we can, God gives us the fuel. The Holy Spirit is water for us to drink. The Holy Spirit is fire to purify us. The Holy Spirit is wind to blow us along on our journey. This doesn't apply to priesthood alone. It could be said of marriage too. Yes, we're called to persevere but let's not forget that it's the Holy Spirit who helps to make it happen.

FOR REFLECTION & DISCUSSION

Have you recognised how the Holy Spirit has helped you to persevere?

'There is an act of will on our part. We need to keep saying 'yes' to Jesus. We have to be careful not to get complacent. We need to invoke the Holy Spirit, but the act of perseverance isn't something that we do in our own strength'.
Discuss

**Song: *You Are Faithful* by Jesus Culture,
featuring Kim Walker-Smith**

16

Contemplating the Holy Trinity

'Go therefore and make disciples of all nations,
baptising them in the name of the
Father and of the Son and of the Holy Spirit.'
Matthew 28:19

SEEING A BIGGER PICTURE

Do you remember the Magic Eye craze of the 1990s? These were 3D pictures 'hidden' in a basic pattern. If you stared long enough at the pattern, training your eyes to look into the pictures, a completely random image would occur. I remember family Christmases where the 'Magic Eye' books would be passed around. We developed a technique of holding the picture right up to our face and slowly pulling it away. After a while there would be a sense of depth in the picture. 'I've got depth!' would be the cry. Then there would be the hope that we could actually work out what the 3D image was without it disappearing.

'I've got depth'. That expression often rings true for me in a deepened awareness of the Holy Trinity. Following my experience in 2011, when I came to understand baptism in the Holy Spirit and received a fresh outpouring and further release of gifts, there seemed to be a new sense of the dynamic nature of the Trinity. This is something that I have heard others attest to when they have had a new awakening to the Holy Spirit's presence. It's as if the picture becomes more alive; sharper.

I think of the Hubble Deep Field image taken by that telescope over ten days in 1995. The telescope was trained on a tiny portion of the sky with only a few stars of the Milky Way visible. As that section of the sky was viewed night after night, it revealed more than 3,000 galaxies, each containing billions of stars. It was a view of the universe going back to its earliest days. Somehow, invoking the Holy Spirit, we can gaze into the depths of the Trinity in a new and exciting way. In doing so, we grow in awareness of how infinite is the love of God. The wonderful mystery of the Trinity is brought that little bit more alive. It feels more real; more personal.

AN EXCITING CONUNDRUM

I think we can all acknowledge how difficult it is to talk about the nature of the Holy Trinity. It's not lost on me that this is the shortest chapter of the book! The apocryphal story of St Augustine on the beach comes to mind. He sees a boy running with a bucket from the sea to a hole he has dug in the sand. He pours water into the hole and goes back again to refill the bucket. Augustine asks him what he's doing and the boy replies that he is trying to get all the water from the sea into the hole. Augustine, touched by the boy's innocence, tells him that he could never fit the magnificence of the ocean into a tiny hole.

The boy replies, 'And you could never understand the Holy Trinity with your limited understanding' and promptly disappears!

Mystery is at the heart of our faith. Mystery isn't something that cannot be understood but is something that always eludes our grasp. It's like a greasy ball which we catch and hold on to for a moment but it still slips through our fingers. As we talk about the Holy Trinity we realise how easy it is to slip into one heresy or another. The Father is not the Son or the Holy Spirit. The Son is not the Father or the Holy Spirit. They are one substance and yet distinct. We are at the limits of language and yet this distinctive revelation of the nature of God is the central truth of Christianity. Jesus reveals this to us. That is why Jesus came.

Jesus, one with Father and the Holy Spirit shows that creation, salvation, the whole divine plan, is the work of the Blessed Trinity. Pouring out the Holy Spirit at Pentecost, this truth comes to reside within us. It is an exciting conundrum.

The Holy Trinity is communion; relationship; an infinite bond of love. Such immense, indescribably creative love exists between the Father and the Son. This bond is the Holy Spirit. It is as if there is a constant breathing in and breathing out of love between the divine Persons. A perpetual self-giving; a non-stop divine dance of celebration which we are called to be caught up in.

There is a beautiful line in the Catechism of the Catholic Church:

> When the Father sends his Word, he always sends his Breath.
>
> In their joint mission, the Son and the Holy Spirit are distinct but inseparable. To be sure, it is Christ who is seen, the visible image of the invisible God, but it is the Spirit who reveals him.
>
> CCC 689

All we can do is bow before the mystery and allow it to possess us.

FOR REFLECTION & DISCUSSION

Reflect on the lines of the Catechism above.

Find a picture of the icon of Rublev - *The Hospitality of Abraham*, where the three figures are considered to be representative of the communion of the Trinity. Meditate on it. What does it say to you?

Spend time with Eucharistic Prayer III (Roman Missal) and reflect on the Trinitarian nature of the liturgy.

Are you beginning to see a bigger picture?

Song: *You Never Let Go* by Matt Redman

17

Hope Springs Eternal

'May the God of hope fill you with all joy and peace in believing, so that you may abound in hope by the power of the Holy Spirit.'
Romans 15:13

THE DANGER OF CYNICISM

'Don't worry Matt. Give it a few years and you'll be cynical like the rest of us.'

Those were words spoken to me by another priest not long after I'd been ordained. I don't remember now who it was and that's probably just as well. I think my 'crime' that day was to have turned up to an event looking a little too cheerful and optimistic! At the time the words really shocked me. I shared this with another priest who had also been recently ordained and he was similarly perturbed by the words. 'That's terrible', he said. 'Make sure you don't go down that road'.

Over the years, with the benefit of reflection, I've come to realise that those words were most probably said in a very tongue-in-cheek manner. However, at the time, what disturbed me was the thought of a priest of Jesus Christ suggesting that pessimism and thus a lack of trust in God would eventually take over; a slip towards despondency; a kind of acknowledgement that evil would somehow win out. I'm not naïve – far from it. I've lived a fair bit. I understand life pretty well, I believe. It's just that sometimes words can really jar, even if they are said in jest.

The irony is that, a good few years on, I can see and understand better what that priest was saying. I'm giving him the benefit of the doubt! I have come to realise that with greater responsibility there is the potential to get swamped, and cynicism can creep in. If one is not careful, though, pessimism might trump optimism and what a sorry state we'd be in then. A parish priest dripping cynicism – perish the thought. That kind of toxic environment is one I would want to steer well clear of.

Where cynicism is concerned, I have seen the potential for this to grow in me where I have experienced a lack of desire for change at different levels; a lack of vision; a lack of engagement. I have seen this try to take root when I have been dragged down by the apathy that is so widespread both inside and outside the Church. I have seen this seek to increase in me when I have been deeply shocked and embarrassed at scandals within the Church. These external frustrations, coupled with inner turmoil, potentially chip away at me, and the insidious nature of cynicism can start to take over. It has to be nipped in the bud, and the Holy Spirit comes to my aid in this regard as I stand up and tell that demon of cynicism to flee in the name of Jesus. It can't and won't get the better of me. The Holy Spirt is my Advocate.

THE VIRTUE OF HOPE

'It's a game changer', said a friend of mine. 'It's an asolute game changer'.

'What is?' I replied. I thought perhaps she was referring to the Video Assistant Referee (VAR) in football or something like that.

'The Holy Spirit is an absolute game changer'. She was referring to the Holy Spirit in all aspects of our lives, not least in bringing us hope and helping us rise above the tendency towards despondency. 'Hope', says St Paul, 'does not disappoint us, because God's love has been poured into our hearts through the Holy Spirit that has been given to us' (Rom 5:5). Hope is a virtue and there is an inextricable link between it and the Holy Spirit. As Jesus ascended to the Father to be our hope, so the Holy Spirit, inseparable from the Father and the Son, has been poured into our hearts. This gift of love naturally brings with it the hope that is Jesus (1 Tim 1:1); a deep certainty that God is with us. As St Paul goes on to say, nothing 'will be able to separate us from the love of God in Christ Jesus our Lord' (Rom 8:39).

In my life as a priest, I have had times where I have been low; times where I have had to deal head on with personal issues; times where there has been a tendency towards feeling somewhat despondent. In the early days, the newness and pressure of ministry brought anxiety. The frustration of being pulled towards areas which don't seem to be in accord with the calling of a priest would drag me down. Feeding into my own issues, this led to some periods of mild depression. It's always been that closeness and awareness of Jesus that has kept me going, though. The recreating breath of the Holy Spirit has always lifted me up; somehow taken me out of the mire and encouraged me forward.

Through baptism we were given a new birth into a 'living hope' through the resurrection of Jesus Christ from the dead' (1 Pt 1:3). That surely is enough to keep us pushing forward. Hope is a wonderful virtue. It comes from beyond the horizon and dwells with us and pulls us towards the horizon. It helps us to be trustful of the pure goodness of God; to be optimistic; to not give in to cynicism - for Jesus loves us. I have continually been encouraged by the living witness of parishioners who have demonstrated this virtue of hope in their lives.

HOPE CAN SET YOU FREE

'Fear can hold you prisoner. Hope can set you free'. That's the tagline to *The Shawshank Redemption,* Stephen King's prison drama which, according to IMDB, is the most popular film of all time. Amazing how a quote from the king of the horror genre can speak so powerfully. Ultimately, fear is not of God. God is love. We know God's love has been poured into our hearts by the Holy Spirit, who communicates Jesus to us. 'Once you were not a people at all, but now you are the people of God' (1 Pt 2:10) we are reminded. This wonderful Word is emblazoned around the font at Clifton Cathedral, the Mother Church of our diocese. Yes, we are the People of God. Jesus is our hope. Let us never forget that and never forget the Holy Spirit, who brings that truth alive.

FOR REFLECTION & DISCUSSION

Do you see how cynicism can get the better of you?

Reflect on the quote from Romans 15:13, from the beginning of the chapter .

'Always be ready to make your defence to anyone who demands from you an accounting for the hope that is in you; yet do it with gentleness and reverence.' 1 Peter 3:15-16
List out your reasons for that hope. Share it with others.

Song: *Jesus Saves* by Tim Hughes

18

Promptings
and Visions

*'When the Spirit of truth comes, he will guide you
into all the truth; for he will not speak on his own,
but will speak whatever he hears, and he will
declare to you the things that are to come.'*
John 16:13

JUST DO IT

'Just do it!' Those were the three words that came firmly
into my mind when I felt the Lord saying I should write this
book. I was at Douai Abbey, the Benedictine monastery
between Newbury and Reading, on retreat.

I had previously announced to the parishes that I wanted
2023 to be a Year of the Holy Spirit within our four parishes.
I had then gone off for a retreat followed by a holiday. I
had browsed around the monastery bookshop and my
eyes alighted on a book called, 'The Holy Spirit and an
Evolving Church' by James Coriden. I decided that was
going to be some background reading for the retreat and
the coming year. It was then that I sensed God saying to
me, 'Write a book about the Holy Spirit'. This hadn't even
been in my consciousness at all. It just sounded clear. 'Write
a book'. It felt exciting and right.

Overnight I had pondered this word, and the next day I was sat in the Blessed Sacrament chapel still considering whether this was really what I was called to do. It was at that moment that I looked down at my feet. A week before I had bought myself some new trainers for going on holiday. They happened to be the Nike brand. Nike's logo is the customary 'tick' and their tagline is 'Just do it'. As I looked at the trainers, those words, 'Just do it!' came into my mind with force. There was a deep sense of the consolation of the Holy Spirit that came with it too. It was clear that I needed to crack on. Rather providentially I had bought a notebook before coming on retreat. I rarely make notes, but perhaps this was part of the bigger plan. The first chapters poured out in a couple of days.

My point with this story is that I have found the Holy Spirit to regularly prompt. I have felt the Holy Spirit regularly help to build vision. I have had very clear commands from the Holy Spirit on a couple of occasions as described earlier in this book. On those occasions I was actually stopped in my tracks. Generally, what I have experienced is the Holy Spirit acting upon my imagination, and using created things, as a way of speaking God's will in my life.

WELCOMED, LOVED, SENT

Another classic example of this is the parish vision statement which we seek to work out of - with varying degrees of success I might add - I wouldn't want to pretend that we've got it right. As a parish leadership team we had prayed about a sentence which might encapsulate our desire for proclaiming Jesus; our desire to give good hospitality and seek to bring belonging; our desire to raise missionary disciples; our desire to reach out to others. All sorts of different formulations were proposed but nothing seemed quite right.

It was when I was on retreat at St Beuno's in North Wales that the answer came to me. I was having a prayerful time. I had sat down and stilled myself, and was seeking to just 'be' in that contemplative way. It then came to me. The words, 'welcomed', 'loved', 'sent' and then 'in the name of Jesus'. I immediately realised this was a gift. This was to be the vision to work out of. 'In the name of Jesus: Welcomed, Loved, Sent'. I simply wrote it down and continued the prayer time. The Holy Spirit had literally dropped this into my lap. Wow! When I returned to the parish, I shared this with Caroline, our outreach worker and Linda, a dear parishioner, and they immediately confirmed the rightness of it.

My experience has been that these promptings and gifts of wider vision have become more apparent as I have been more aware of the importance of invoking the Holy Spirit. It all seems to have flowed a great deal more since 2011 and all that happened through the Life in the Spirit Seminars. It's what happened with the New Awakenings Mission Team as discussed in an earlier chapter. The prompt came as I was gazing on a stained-glass window of the Holy Spirit. The prompt was shared and confirmed and the rest followed. Even the name 'New Awakenings' came clearly into my mind on another occasion. If something is of the Holy Spirit the way forward is cleared. Supporters come; money comes if needed; the deep sense of interconnectedness talked about elsewhere in this book increases.

ONE VISION

It's not just big prompts that come our way. There are so many other little inspirations. Some of these are just the natural firing of synapses in the brain in order to live life. Others are clearly thoughts put there by the Holy Spirit in order to push forward with the mission in whatever baby steps might be appropriate. Oh, how many of these I have missed or not heeded. Perhaps that's why there are louder shouts at times! A notebook is really useful in this regard. If it's super-important (sorry for the modern parlance), though, the Holy Spirit will get through.

I guess anyone reading this might well say, 'Well all this is pretty obvious to us. Isn't this the experience of all Christians?' Well, yes, it may well be, but I haven't heard it articulated a great deal. All I am doing is being faithful in sharing what I've been prompted to do. I'm sure there are millions of Jesus' followers who have far more clarity over promptings and visions. I'm simply acting out of a prompting I have had. I believe that being open to the graces of our Baptism and Confirmation, being further unbound in us, may increase this in many. I wonder whether the Holy Spirit is knocking at the door but many of us are not listening or not quite in tune.

Jesus is amazing. His Lordship over my life is all that matters, even though I err. His Lordship over me is heightened when I am open to the gifts of the Holy Spirit. Promptings become clearer; vision is widened. Something that comes to me about vision is that the true test is whether it brings about unity. The Holy Spirit may disturb for sure. We need, at times, to be shaken out of complacency. Ultimately, though, the Holy Spirit seeks to bring that same unity which is God. The Father, Son and Holy Spirit are one. The dynamism of the Trinity that sends us in the name of Jesus, in the power of the Spirit, also pulls us together. The acid test for any prompting or developing vision is whether it builds up the People of God, brings increase, and a deeper sense of belonging and unity.

I also find promptings and inspirations coming from all sorts of different places, be it film, TV, song lyrics, etc. These can all be turned to the good for the sake of proclaiming the Gospel. So perhaps the last word goes to Queen and Freddie Mercury, 'I had a dream when I was young, a dream of sweet illusion, a glimpse of hope and unity, and visions of one sweet union. One man, one goal, one mission, one God. One vision!'

Praise you Jesus!

FOR REFLECTION & DISCUSSION

Have you ever had clear promptings from the Holy Spirit?

What is the Holy Spirit prompting you to do at this particular time in your life?

Song: *Jesus Loves Me* by Chris Tomlin

19

The Wonder
of Creation

*'In the beginning when God created the heavens
and the earth, the earth was a formless void and
darkness covered the face of the deep, while
a wind swept over the face of the water.'*
Gen 1: 1-2

RISING SUN OR RISEN SON?
'Welcome to the land of the Rising Sun', I thought, as I flew
into Japan at the beginning of February 2000.

I had been baptised in the Holy Spirit a few weeks earlier
and had come to a new and personal relationship with
Jesus. The gifts of the Holy Spirit had come alive in me. I
had been in Singapore for a business meeting and caught
a late-night flight to Tokyo, a seven-hour journey. I was
buzzing with the Holy Spirit. This faith; this new awareness
of love; this call to step out in discipleship was so exciting
but I still had my job to do.

As we were in the air, about an hour from our destination,
the sun started to come up. This was the most spectacular
sight I have ever seen. Everyone else on the plane
appeared to be asleep, tucked up with blankets, and
many had eye masks on. How could they not be seeing

this? I thought, filled with wonder. I couldn't see anyone with their eyes open and yet there was an amazing scene panning out in the sky around us – the sun was rising. This was how I described it at the time in a diary:

> From the near blackness, above, the sky came down to the horizon in lightening hues of blue. From the deepest, darkest blue to the beautiful sky blue of a summer's day, all sat atop a hazy layer of greenish swirly mist, wisping its way over sand, then terracotta and rust, firmly placed over a base of deep ruddy brown. The effect would change, but not to the watching eye. Then, as we approached the coast of Japan, the sun appeared as the bright, fiery giant we know, and shortly after came up a beautifully reddish pink with the fluffy clouds mirroring this with an indescribable pinkish tinge. Welcome to the land of the Rising Sun!

The gift of wonder had really been stirred in me. I have always appreciated the beauty of nature. I lived in Lancaster for a couple of years in the mid-1990s, not far from the Lake District, and that majestic scenery was certainly appreciated by me. Yet, the wonder that I was experiencing as I flew into Japan that day seemed different. It was is if I was in relationship with what I was seeing before me. It was like a religious experience; there was a connectedness, and I was being spoken to at a deep level, in the Spirit, by the Risen Son.

When I look at your heavens, the work of your fingers, the moon and the stars that you have established; what are human beings that you are mindful of them, mortals that you care for them?
Psalm 8:3-4

BREATH

'I love you to the moon and back' is an expression often used to try and convey the depth of one's feeling for another. The moon is pretty far relative to distances on the earth and so the sentiment is well understood. The utter immensity of God's creation, on the other hand, is really too much for our minds to take in. It almost blows my mind to consider that there are more stars in the universe than there are grains of sand on our planet. Conversely, there are more molecules in a couple of tablespoons of water than there are stars. From the staggering size of the Universe, to the tiniest particle, our breath should be taken away by the wonder of it all.

Breath is an important word when it comes to creation. The Holy Spirit is the Breath. Whilst our Creed states that all things came into being through the Word of God, and thus all creation is shot through with Christ, the Breath was always there with the Father and the Word in this creative adventure. This means that all of creation is marked with the stamp of the Blessed Trinity. This is not to say that God is in creation; we don't worship trees, rivers or mountains. What we can say is that we discover something of God in the created order. Is that why the Holy Spirit's gift of wonder can abound in us and flood us with joy when we enter into some kind of relationship with nature? Is that why the same sense of wonder and deep respect can abound in us as we look upon each other as temples of the Spirit? The divine Breath oozes all around us and we, as conscious and sensate beings, marked with the Trinity, can really appreciate it. We rejoice in it – but it needs to make a difference.

RELATIONSHIP

I have often thought how easy it is to become desensitised to suffering. From wars to natural disasters to mindless shootings. We see so much bad news on the television that it is all too straightforward to simply change channels. It seems much harder for us to be shocked by the senseless violence and injustice that is all around. This is the same with the climate crisis and the terrifying effect that this is having on communities around the world, especially the poorest, and the potential catastrophe that awaits future generations. How do we stop that slide into apathy? How are our eyes going to be opened and then stay focused? A deeper conversion of heart is required.

Fanning into a flame the gifts of the Holy Spirit makes a huge difference here. The Holy Spirit opens our eyes and inspires that wonder in us. The Holy Spirit brings us to realise how we are in relationship with all people and the whole of creation. We come to see Christ in all. The Holy Spirit never lets go and keeps helping us to return to what is important so that complacency needn't be a worry.

My travels in export sales took me to many countries. They made me realise how we are all the same as human beings. This was well before the gifts of the Holy Spirit were ignited in me. That truth needs to come more fully alive in all of us so that a deeper appreciation of our interconnectedness grows; so that there is wonder and awe which builds relationship. Similarly, we need to deepen our appreciation of the connection with the whole of the created order, to bring about an ecological conversion; a new vision; a renewed purpose to reorder our lives for the sake of the cosmos and our place in it. Surely our very earthly existence depends on it. Come Holy Spirit, just do it in us!

FOR REFLECTION & DISCUSSION

Describe a landscape or something which engenders in you great wonder and awe. Give thanks for it.

Reflect on the notion of 'breath' as the creative force – the Holy Spirit – as seen at the beginning of creation and hovering over Mary.

Watch 'The Letter' - www.theletterfilm.org – this is Pope Francis' call to see how everything is interconnected, so that we might come to a deeper appreciation of our role in creation.
Ask the Holy Spirit to open your heart and mind to what is being offered.

Song: *What a Beautiful Name* by Hillsong Worship

20

Fire, Water, and Dove

'Divided tongues, as of fire, appeared among them, and a tongue rested on each of them. All of them were filled with the Holy Spirit.'
Acts 2:3

READY FOR LAUNCH?

'5-4-3-2-1. We have lift off'. Those are words I've heard on many an occasion as I'm a bit of rocket geek. I love watching rocket launches. How amazing to watch replays of the Saturn V rockets launching the Apollo missions. Now we have the even more powerful NASA Space Launch System rockets and Space-X's Starship launch vehicle and other amazing craft. I'd love to see one taking off for real. The mighty power of those engines igniting and the awesome sight of the rocket clearing the tower, with the deafening roar and the majestic fire. The incredible propulsion and build-up of speed. It sends a tingle down my spine. It makes something in me well up. It is a mini-wonder. A man-made wonder, harnessing the gifts of creation.

What a discovery fire must have been for our ancestors. To make fire and contain it. To tame it, so to speak. But we know fire never wants to be contained. It will always seek to spread. We see the tragedy of house fires; the devastation wrought by forest fires. Fire as a symbol of the Holy Spirit is so powerful because it represents God's energy. It is a wildfire of pure love. A transforming energy that cannot be quelled and which, by its very nature, is always life-giving. Even as it burns down barriers; challenges individuals; it is always bringing unity, always directing us towards Jesus and the burning love of the Trinity.

John the Baptist proclaims Christ as the one who will baptise with the Holy Spirt and fire (Luke 3:16). Jesus himself says he has come to bring fire to the earth (Luke 12:49). This is the fire of purification. The fire of division and judgement which will ultimately bring unity. It is an image loaded with symbolism, expressive of an active, dynamic Spirit. At Pentecost the Holy Spirit appears as tongues of fire (Acts 2:3) and fulfils the prophecy of John the Baptist. 'Ready for launch!' The Holy Spirit shoots us into the stratosphere but never leaves us.

WATER, WATER EVERYWHERE

The deepest part of the Pacific Ocean, Challenger Deep, is over seven miles deep. That idea almost frightens me to death. To imagine going in a submersible to the sea-bed with seven miles of water above me. The immensity of the oceans astounds me. The danger steers me clear of it. Even fresh water has its major perils. High waterfalls, white water rapids. They look amazing but don't let me get too close. I respect those who make their living in these environments, but it's not for me.

Water is death-dealing and life-giving. We look at the story of the Flood. The Exodus story too, with the parted waters offering safe passage, and the returning waters cascading in on the advancing army of Pharaoh (Exodus 14). Symbols of God's protective power and God's doing away with sin and evil. Signs of how water will become a source of new life through the death and resurrection of Christ. Water as the sign of baptism. The font being a symbol of the watery womb where we grew and where we now receive birth given to us in the Holy Spirit.

How refreshing a slug of water is on a hot day. The feeling of refreshment when we feel so parched. Even those close to dehydration are quickly revived as water is poured into them. Water is such a powerful image of the life-giving qualities of the Holy Spirit. How we enjoy standing under a powerful shower or plunging into a bath or pool. Being immersed, covered with water in a safe fashion. This is the kind of imagery which helps us to appreciate the all-encompassing and enwrapping love of God in Christ. The water of the Holy Spirit wells up within us and quenches our thirst. The Holy Spirit is freshly poured over us and, if we can believe it, this is a constant torrent. Water, like fire, cannot be fully contained.

On the Cross, blood and water flow from the side of Jesus as symbols of the grace of the sacraments; the forgiveness that comes from Christ through baptism and is lavished upon us through the Holy Spirit (John 19:34). Just as Ezekiel had a vision of the water flowing from the temple bringing life (Ezk 47), so the Holy brings that life to the children of God.

'Like a fire, like a flood, come however you want' sing the worship band. They sing of how the Holy Spirit tears down walls; fills us with power; rebuilds us. Heaven has come to earth in Jesus Christ, and he has poured out fire and water over the whole of creation through the event of Pentecost.

THE DOVE AND OTHER SYMBOLS
It is said that birds of a feather flock together. It is an impressive sight to witness the flocking of starlings, so called 'murmurations'. There is a sense of grace about their pulsating formations. Humans have always been fascinated with bird flight. We hanker after the wonder of being able to soar high above the earth with a wide vista. We wonder at the incredible migrations of birds as they fly half way around the world.

The image of the Holy Spirit as a dove is a traditional one. Noah sent out the dove after the Flood, and it returned with a freshly plucked olive leaf as a sign of the habitability of the earth and the flourishing of life (Gen 8:6-12). The Flood was a symbol of baptism and the new life brought by the Holy Spirit. In the Gospels, the Holy Spirit descends upon Jesus at his baptism in the form of a dove, so this is an important image. The dove flies where it wishes, just as the Holy Spirit does. It ascends; soars; hovers; descends. It always seeks to bring about unity among the children of God.

There are other symbols of the Holy Spirit variously discussed in this book. We see how Jesus is 'anointed' by the Holy Spirit at his baptism (chapter 8). This is a lavish symbol of privilege and love. The psalmist gives the beautiful image, taken from Exodus, of the oil on the head of Aaron running down upon his beard and onto his robes (Ps 133:1-2). Oil, like water, runs where it will. Oil is a lubricant too. As well as anointing it loosens bonds; helps things to move; greases the wheels. In the Sacraments of the Church, Chrism is the highest oil of anointing. It has a sweet perfume, another sensory reminder of the goodness of God.

I have already shared thoughts on the Holy Spirit, the Breath – the wind; that gentle breeze or mighty gust, that blows wherever it will. I suggest some others below, that you might reflect on, so that we don't forget the Holy Spirit. We may see some of our own. I give the last word to the worship band. Yes, this is Jesus' love for us. He is fiercely in love with us, and the Holy Spirit communicates it to us through so many symbols.

Like a tidal wave crashing over me, rushing in to meet me here – your love is fierce. Like a hurricane that I can't escape, tearing through the atmosphere – your love is fierce.

FOR REFLECTION & DISCUSSION

Discuss the images of the Holy Spirit and consider what they are saying about the action of God in our lives.

Look at image of the Holy Spirit as 'cloud' (Exodus 33:9; Luke 21:27; Acts 1:9)

Reflect on the image of the Holy Spirit as 'the seal', which is closely linked to anointing. The indelible mark left on us. See 2 Cor 1:21-22.

'Come Holy Spirit!' Keep that mantra going in your mind and let it move to your heart more and more.

Song: *Living With a Fire* by Jesus Culture

21

Gratefulness

'be filled with the Spirit.....
giving thanks to God the Father
at all times and for everything
in the name of our Lord Jesus Christ.'
Ephesians 5:18-20

THE SILVER JUBILARIAN

'Gratitude and simplicity. These have been the mainstays during my ministry', said the priest at St Austin and St Gregory Church in Margate. I was in the area on holiday and had dropped into Sunday Mass there. It happened to be the Solemnity of the Assumption of the Blessed Virgin Mary. The parish still had a lot of Covid-19 measures in place and I sat there in that rather surreal environment, which we all had got accustomed to, with face-covering on and hazard tape everywhere.

The priest was speaking at the end of Mass, thanking parishioners who had celebrated with him his silver jubilee of Ordination a few days earlier. He just happened to mention about the gift of priesthood and said that 'gratitude' and 'simplicity' had always been at the heart of his life and ministry. Those words really spoke to me. I wrote them down. I love the image of simplicity –

not allowing life to get too complex and relying on God, who is not complex at all. There's a great grace in letting go, and I'm sure the Holy Spirit is on hand to assist in this regard. I see so much complexity in the life and relationships of people around me. So many are weighed down by it. The Holy Spirit can cut through that. To live life simply is to hand yourself over to God and let so much that could easily weigh us down just wash over us. There must be another chapter here just on simplicity!

GRATITUDE

As a novice with The Redemptorists, I had the opportunity to read a good many books. It was a whole spiritual year, a real blessing. We were encouraged to read a lot. Naturally I read many spiritual classics but also loads of classic fiction. At one point in the year our Novice Master, Fr Sean, also chose particular books for each of the five of us. He asked us to read them and have spiritual chats with him about them. The book he chose for me was *Gratefulness: The Heart of Prayer* by Brother David Steindl-Rast. Can I remember much of the details about it? No. However, there was something about that book that really touched my heart. Ever since, I've had a deeper appreciation of the centrality of gratefulness in prayer. We are a eucharistic people. The very word means 'thanksgiving'. Thanksgiving is at the core of who we are as the People of God. The Holy Spirit brings this alive.

As children, a spirit of gratitude was engendered in me and my two sisters by our parents. We were always taught to be polite, to say 'please' and 'thank you' and not to be shy in this respect. After Christmas and birthdays we were expected to write 'thank you' letters to grandparents, aunts and uncles for gifts received. It became like second nature. I would like to think that I have always shown gratitude to others throughout my life. The spirit of gratitude certainly increased in me, though, after my meeting with Christ and the enlivening of the gifts of the Holy Spirit within.

Gratitude increases in us when we have a greater connection with the giver. A mystery donor may give us a great gift and we will be extremely grateful. How much better does it feel actually to be able to thank the donor in person? We sometimes see this on television when someone meets another person who saved their life. The actual connection makes all the difference.

God in Christ has given us the gift of salvation. It is on offer to all. Some may shrug and say, 'That's nice. Whatever'. But when, in faith, we accept this gift, the desire to give thanks comes alive. When we allow a personal relationship with Jesus to grow and become very real with the Holy Spirit's impetus, thanksgiving takes on a new level. There is a connectedness; relationship; our 'thank you' becomes a one-to-one conversation.

I'D LIKE TO THANK...
We've all watched award ceremonies such as The Oscars. We've heard those gushy acceptance speeches by famous actors and directors. They are always replete with

thanks for those who have helped on the journey. How often do we sit back and reflect on all those for whom we owe so much and to whom we ought to be grateful? During the pandemic lockdowns there were regular 'Claps for Carers'. A spirit of gratitude was sought to be engendered in the population for those on the frontline. We are inter-connected and there are so many near to us and seemingly far from us for whom we can be grateful.

The Holy Spirit showers us with many gifts. As our eyes are opened more widely to this, the natural reaction is to give praise and thanks. Sometimes we need a new awakening in this regard. An on-going audit of what has come our way, is coming our way, and keeps coming our way from God is a great idea. The Holy Spirit can do this for us. The Holy Spirit shows us who and what to be thankful for in our lives. The Holy Spirit can reveal so much that we take for granted. The Holy Spirit presents our thanks to the God-head. God doesn't need our thanks but, recognising our utter dependence on God and God's great goodness, the Holy Spirit fires up this personal spirit of gratefulness. It's the natural reaction of one who truly understands their relationship with the author, creator and redeemer of our lives.

In our parishes, I hope I give a good example of being a grateful person. Being called to lead is something that needs to be done in humility and with gratitude for all those who put their gifts at the service of the People of God. I'm always careful when giving public thanks to individuals because I'm afraid of missing someone out!

Whenever I start a time of personal prayer, I always give praise to God; seek forgiveness for my shortcomings, and then give thanks for the gift of being in relationship with God. The rest flows from there. I seek to make gratefulness the heart of my prayer just as it is at the heart of our liturgical prayer. Thanks be to God. It really is that simple.

'O give thanks to the Lord, for he is good;
for his steadfast love endures forever.'
Psalm 106:1

FOR REFLECTION & DISCUSSION

Are you a thankful person? What are you especially thankful for?

'Thank you Jesus. Thank you Jesus. Thank you Lord for loving me.
'Thank you Jesus. Thank you Jesus. Thank you Lord for loving me.'
Sing it!

Song: *Thank You Jesus* by Hillsong Worship

22

Perpetual
Pentecost

'I will extol you, my God and King,
and bless your name forever and ever.
Every day I will bless you,
and praise your name for ever and ever.
Great is the Lord, and greatly to be praised;
his greatness is unsearchable.'
Psalm 145:1-3

CHRISTMAS AND EASTER EVERY DAY?

I Wish It Could Be Christmas Everyday by Wizzard is one of those classic Christmas songs that ends up as an earworm for six weeks or so each year. Whatever shop or pub you go into, you're bound to hear it at some point. 'Well I wish it could be Christmas every day, when the kids start singing and the band begins to play'. It's rather addictive like so many Christmas pop songs. We can all understand the sentiment. Christmas is a magical time. There is a special atmosphere at this time of year whether you're a believer or non-believer. For Christians, celebrating the Incarnation; the Word made Flesh; Jesus, our Lord and Saviour is an incredible joy. God made man; true God from true God; consubstantial with the Father – he appears in human history, a light to the nations. Yes, it's fair to say that it would be great to celebrate Christmas every day and revel in this truth.

Easter, of course, is the greatest feast of the whole year. Christ is our Passover. He is the one who, obedient to the Father and the Holy Spirit, continued faithfully in his proclamation of the Kingdom of God to death. Through his death and resurrection we have new life in him. His is the perfect sacrifice. He is the priest, victim and lamb of sacrifice. The Cross is his altar. Through his steadfast love and self-offering we are free from the power of sin and the devil over us. Death has no sting. Heaven is flung open. Jesus is victorious, and we celebrate this especially every Sunday. Every Sunday is a special celebration of the day of Resurrection. Every day we live by the light of Easter.

PENTECOST EVERY DAY?

That light of Easter that lifts our hearts in praise. Those eyes we are given to see who the child is in the manger at Christmas. These are gifts of the Holy Spirit poured out at Pentecost. The Holy Spirit, sent by Father and Son and making the God-head real to us, enlightens our hearts and minds to the truth and gives us spiritual sight. This same Holy Spirit allows us to be drawn into deep relationship with the Holy Trinity. The Holy Spirit graces us and empowers us as fervent disciples of Jesus; communicators of the Father's love. We are able to say 'Jesus is Lord' as a result, and preach the Good News with power. This all happens as the Paschal Mystery is brought to life in our consciousness through the Ascension of Christ, and through the ensuing promised outpouring of the Holy Spirit at Pentecost. Pentecost is such a wonderful feast. We want Christmas every day; Easter every day; logically therefore we should want Pentecost every day.

The basic premise of this book has been that the Holy Spirit is so often seen as the forgotten Person of the Holy Trinity. Previous Popes have alluded to this. Many great commentators have said the same. The Catechism of the Catholic Church even has a section about 'Speaking about the Holy Spirit'. Here it is acknowledged that the Holy Spirit has no face, and that how many still find it difficult to communicate the vital presence of the Holy Spirit. It goes on to acknowledge how the fundamentals of our faith would be totally stripped away without the Holy Spirit's very real role and presence. Jesus is the one we want to, and must, proclaim. The Holy Spirit is there to help and guide through the gifts.

Reflecting on all of this, I have sometimes wondered if we are impoverished in our celebrations of the Holy Spirit within the liturgical life of the Church. Pentecost is the supreme festival of the Holy Spirit, but what about the rest of the year? Perhaps it's all about getting the right mindset. I was praying the Prayer of the Church the other day and the following two verses struck me from the Office of Readings:

> *This day the Lord for sinners slain*
> *In might victorious rose again:*
> *O Jesus, may we raised be*
> *From death of sin to life in thee!*

This day the Holy Spirit came
With fiery tongues of cloven flame:
O Spirit, fill our hearts this day
With grace to hear and grace to pray.

What came to me was that Sunday is the day of Resurrection, clearly. It is also the day of Pentecost. In fact, because the Trinity is truly inseparable, every day, every celebration honours all three Persons of the Trinity. If we want a specific focus on the Holy Spirit, it is up to us to draw that out. For example, the Baptism of the Lord is clearly an opportunity to concentrate on the action of the Holy Spirit. What about the feasts of Mary, our beautiful mother, which I will ponder in the final chapter? There are many references to the action of the Holy Spirit in Jesus' life. The Acts of the Apostles is really a testimony to the power of the Holy Spirit, and St Paul is not shy in sharing about the Spirit too. Let's not forget the references and allusion to the work of the Holy Spirit in the Old Testament. These all need to be drawn out to give people the opportunity to more deeply know Christ, and the power of the Holy Spirit, spread forth across the universe.

Even more than this, if we are to perpetuate the memory of Jesus Christ through all generations, then let us speak clearly of the Father's love and the work of the Holy Spirit in all celebrations. We are Christians. Christians live by the teaching of Christ and live life in the Spirit. Let us draw out the dynamism of the mystery in order to fulfil our mandate of proclamation.

PENTECOST CELEBRATIONS

My first serious celebration of Pentecost was in June 2000, following my experience of baptism in the Holy Spirit earlier that year. I remember going to an ecumenical celebration at The County Ground, home of Swindon Town (there hasn't been much rejoicing there for a few years!) It was an eye-opener for me because I had never come together with other Christians, apart from one time. When my dad worked in Saudi Arabia, his faith seemed to flourish as he joined a Christian fellowship. I actually wonder whether he might have been baptised in the Holy Spirit when he was there as his faith seemed to take off when he returned to the UK. We went along to a meeting in the Baptist church when he came back home for good, but mum and dad quickly realised that they felt our home was in the Catholic Church.

I remember that Pentecost celebration at the County Ground well. There was still great excitement in me at that time; a huge sense of consolation. I recall the lively singing and big flags waving. It was a truly special occasion. For me it begs the question as to why I didn't really experience anything quite like that again until 2011. It also makes me realise that I haven't always given enough pastoral priority to this celebration in the parishes. Perhaps this is why I am saying that, with the Holy Spirit directing, a better balance can be sought throughout the year to draw out the fullness of the mystery without putting all the pressure on one day.

There was one major Pentecost-like moment that I recall

back in 2006. I went to Honduras for a mission experience with the Redemptorists. I was staying at a mission station right out in the middle of nowhere in a place called Trojes. From there I went off on a mule (not a pretty sight!) to stay with a family in a far-flung tiny desperately poor settlement. We were somewhere in the region of El Paraíso. The community would gather regularly for prayer in a tiny little chapel. A priest might visit once or twice a year to celebrate the Eucharist as there were over a hundred small churches dotted around a vast area. They would gather around the Word of God and then they would start praying out loud and praising in tongues. It got very loud and the presence of the Holy Spirit was tangible. I remember taking it in my stride as it all seemed very natural. This was the only time I had experienced anything like this since 2000 and wouldn't again until 2011. I have to say, though, that I've never quite felt the intensity that I felt that day when I was with those materially poor, but spiritually rich, joyful souls in Trojes.

HEARTS ON FIRE

One way that I have found to keep a focus on the Holy Spirit has been through some experiences of Churches Together, and the ecumenical movement. In one of the parishes I serve in Bristol, the local Baptist church and three Church of England parishes would come together with ourselves under the banner 'Hearts on Fire'. As ministers, we all found common ground in a passion for Jesus and a shared charismatic spirituality. We put on several praise and worship sessions over the space of a couple of years in each other's churches. It was a great way to explore our shared desire to proclaim Jesus as Lord, and to be open to the gifts of the Holy Spirit. Covid-19 and a change of personnel have meant this has tailed off, but it was a good season and there are plenty of embers to blow on. I always remember one of the ministers, who came to one of our planning meetings downcast. His parish had been giving him an appraisal. One had told him, 'You talk too much about Jesus and not enough about the Church'. He'd felt deflated by that. We assured him, that was his badge of honour!

PONDER THE LITURGY

The Church's liturgy is a great gift that has been handed on to us. With the Holy Spirit enflaming our hearts and fanning into a flame the gifts, we can come to see that truth. We seek the face of Christ within the liturgy. The Holy Spirit assists. Making the sign of the Cross slowly can lead to a deep meditation on the mystery of who God is. Especially during the eucharistic prayer, let us listen carefully to the words being prayed. Real, active participation is what we are called to. The Trinitarian dynamism of the prayers is really powerful. Everything is a dialogue with the Father in the power of the Holy Spirit, with Jesus being present to us. With the gift of imagination and enlightened hearts we can make it Christmas, Easter and Pentecost every day. So, don't forget the Holy Spirit in order to make it happen.

FOR REFLECTION & DISCUSSION

How do you keep alive that awareness of the Holy Spirit in you each day?

Reflect on your desire for a fresh outpouring of the Holy Spirit. Talk about it with others.

'Come Holy Spirit'! Say each word slowly and keep repeating.

Song: *Heaven is Here* by Jesus Culture

23

Vocation

'The next day Jesus decided to go to Galilee.
He found Philip and said to him, 'Follow me.'
John 1:43

A DREAM IN THE HEART

'I just wanna be part of your symphony' sings Zara Larsson on Clean Bandit's pop song of the same name. 'I just wanna be part of your symphony, will you hold me tight and not let go?' That sounds like a good request to make to the Holy Spirit, who conducts the symphony that is the Church, the People of God. Those who follow Jesus are part of a missionary Church which gathers the natural gifts of all its faithful and puts them to good use. When this works well, it is like a beautiful symphony. When we understand that we are held tight, never abandoned, we can truly flourish. Following Jesus closely, we become fervent disciples and discover our particular vocation.

It is sometimes said that there is a dream in the heart of God for every human being. God has known from the beginning of time the gifts bestowed upon us and how these can be put to good use. I am speaking here of our natural gifts and talents. Through Baptism and Confirmation, a vocation has been sown into our hearts by the Holy Spirit; a calling for us to discover under the guidance of the same Holy Spirit. This is the dream planted within us, which we are to uncover as we follow Jesus. The Holy Spirit enables us to put our natural gifts to the use of the service of the mission of Christ's Church. The Holy Spirit further graces us with the gifts described in chapter 9, not least the gift of courage to move forward in confidence.

I'm not a musician but I can see how an orchestra comes together to make a beautiful sound when each member knows their role. Each member with their instrument is like a vocation being lived out to the full. When all the musicians are playing together, according to the script provided, then the result is something beautiful; majestic.

DEEPENING DISCIPLESHIP

There are many ways that we can put our natural gifts to the service of others. There are so many paths of service to each other and the whole world. When we speak of vocation, though, we are talking in this context of a calling to a particular state of life. It is important to remember that the primary vocation of every human being is to love, just as God is love! Following on from this, there is a vocation to either marriage, consecrated life, priesthood or the single life. From these states of life may flow other callings; different forms of work or careers; other ways of serving God and the whole of humanity. Ultimately, though, the Holy Spirit sows in the hearts of all the faithful a vocation, a calling to a particular state of life.

I had the privilege of serving as Diocesan Vocations Director for seven years from 2012-2019. In this time, I was tasked with trying to build a 'culture of vocation' within our parishes. We forget the importance of communicating about vocation at our peril. A Church that is really alive is one where its members are discerning deeply their vocation. When vocations flourish it is a sign of the Holy Spirit truly at work and of a people deepening in their discipleship. Those who come to a deeper faith in Jesus naturally open themselves to discernment and begin to listen attentively to the Spirit's prompting.

This 'culture of vocation' can only be built by invoking the guidance and empowerment of the Holy Spirit. We need to assist people in their following of Jesus and to help them deepen their discipleship. It's not good enough just to put out a poster campaign telling everyone they have a vocation. There is the need for discipleship training and places where people can gather to talk about their journey following Jesus. It's important for people to hear vocation stories. It's necessary to create a space where people can listen to what the Holy Spirit is saying to them. Another word for 'listening', could be 'leaning in'. We rest with Jesus. We quieten our hearts and we 'lean in' to him so that we hear the prompting and guidance of the Holy Spirit coming from within. This is where discernment begins.

COURAGE
All the gifts of the Holy Spirit are to be put to use for helping us to discover our vocation. That is why we should seek to

foster baptism in the Holy Spirit. Courage is one particular gift which is really valuable. We need to step out in faith and explore with courage. I think this is particularly true where a young man or woman might sense a calling to the religious life or to the priesthood. It is important to explore this. If this is your calling then it will become apparent. If it is not your calling then as one door closes another will open. It would be a tragedy if people were missing out on their vocation because of fear of failure. There's no such thing as failure when we follow Jesus to the best of our ability and listen to the Holy Spirit by venturing out in faith.

We also need to be courageous in our encouragement and accompaniment of the younger members of our parishes. We need the Holy Spirit's assistance here for sure. Younger people are often conspicuous by their absence from the regular liturgical life of the parish. So often I hear parishioners ask, 'Why aren't we doing more for young people?' My question is always, 'What are you doing?' We're all in this together. The Church is alive when, empowered by the Holy Spirt and fervent in our love for Jesus we all step up to the plate. Discerning, knowing, owning our vocation – when that's really happening we are truly part of God's great symphony.

FOR REFLECTION & DISCUSSION

How aware are you of your vocation? Are you able to communicate about vocation with others?

What do you do to encourage younger people in their faith?

Do you 'lean in' and listen to the Holy Spirit? What is the Holy Spirit saying now?

Song: *Prince of Peace* by Hillsong United

24

Priesthood
and the Holy Spirit

'You did not choose me but I chose you.
And I appointed you to go out and bear fruit,
fruit that will last.'
John 15:16

DEEPEST DESIRE
'PRIESTHOOD'
'YOU SHALL BE A PRIEST'
These are the words that came to me in an instant in January 2000. I had acknowledged the Holy Spirit was guiding me. This led to me immediately being baptised in the Holy Spirit with a profound encounter with my Lord and Saviour, Jesus Christ. It was the start of a new journey and I haven't looked back.

I have always felt strongly that I was called to be a priest from that day forward. When I was being asked by the Holy Spirit to make the decision to leave religious life with the Redemptorists, I had to put the call on hold for a time in order to be free to make the decision. It soon came back though, and I was encouraged to keep moving forward.

The crystallisation of my calling to the priesthood came in 2007. I had gone back to seminary, this time in formation for the diocesan priesthood. There was a little anxiety in me. Having had to make the decision to leave the Redemptorists, I was worried about being presented with another big decision. Perhaps there was a little less clarity about my calling to the priesthood at that moment in time. This meant I needed to deepen my prayer and closeness to Jesus. My Spiritual Director, Fr Gerard Bradley, encouraged me to read *New Seeds of Contemplation by* Thomas Merton. In that book he talks about how we can discover God's will insofar as we discover our deepest desire. I was ruminating on this idea at home during the half term break. Mum and dad were out. It was peaceful, and I was sat in the conservatory looking out at the garden. I asked God to help me to discover that deepest desire, and it became abundantly clear that it was to serve Jesus Christ as a priest. It's hard to really explain. I was definitely on the right track. It was a joyful, touchstone moment and I realised that I could move forward in hope and that this would happen.

THE ACTION OF THE HOLY SPIRIT
'Ooh, I love being a priest', exclaims Dougal to Fr Ted with a wide-eyed, daft grin on his face. I wouldn't want to sound quite like that, but I do love being a priest. It is a great joy. It is pure gift. My priesthood is a gift from God to me, and to and for the People of God. In the words of St John Paul II, I'm an ordinary man called to an extraordinary task. I'm a priest of Jesus Christ called to preach, teach and sanctify in his name.

The Holy Spirit is central to my ministry, naturally. As a minister of Jesus Christ, sharing in his high priesthood, the Holy Spirit is constantly there, for theirs is a common mission. In the Rite of Ordination, prior to my consecration, the bishop prayed, with hands outstretched over me as a symbol of the outpouring of the Holy Spirit:

> Hear us, Lord our God, and pour out upon this servant of yours the blessing of the Holy Spirit and the grace and power of the priesthood.

He anointed my hands and said:

> The Father anointed our Lord Jesus Christ through the power of the Holy Spirit. May Jesus preserve you to sanctify the Christian people and to offer sacrifice to God.

Yes, just as all the baptised share in the anointing of Jesus through baptism, the ministerial priest is intimately bonded to Christ the High Priest. He is set apart to offer the Sacrifice of the Mass; to forgive sins in the person of Christ; to proclaim the Word of Life in the liturgy. Just as Christ's greatest gift was to impart the Holy Spirit upon the apostles, so the priest shares in a particular way with this ministry of further outpouring.

In chapter 2, I talked about how I saw the action of the Holy Spirit in the Eucharist one day as another priest was celebrating Mass. My hands became hot as I celebrated my first Mass. The Holy Spirit wanted to confirm His presence; his action. This action of the Holy Spirit is constantly at work in the priest to renew him, give him new vision, help him to see how God is working in and around him. The priest, open to the Holy Spirit, is able to listen carefully, discern well, receive promptings and build vision. Open to the gifts of the Holy Spirit, he can speak prophetic words, receive insight, heal. I have found this awareness of the presence of the Holy Spirit in my ministry as I have sought to draw closer to Jesus, and as I have invoked the Spirit. We need to ask.

SEMINARY

Two years after I was ordained priest, I was asked to serve as university chaplain at the Catholic Chaplaincy in Bristol. This was a great privilege. The building was in a poor state and had not been looked after properly. I quickly learnt how priests get dragged down by issues around buildings and such like. It drained my energy. One property surveyor told me that he thought all seminaries should teach a course in property management. 'No!' I exclaimed. 'Surely not.' Another said, 'You're not priests really, you're more like business managers'. 'Aargh. How terrible. Yet how insightful', I thought. Some priests have gifts in these areas, but I can't see that this is what I was called to do, or any priest for that matter. Preach, teach, sanctify. Let the priests be priests.

If there were something I would recommend being taught in the seminary, it would be a deeper appreciation of the role of the Holy Spirit. I don't remember any 'pneumatology' (fancy word for the study of the Holy Spirit!). Also, an exploration of and openness to the gifts of the Holy Spirit should be encouraged, especially the charismatic gifts. How could it be that in six years of formation for the priesthood, these were never discussed; never encouraged. They are there to build faith; to build up the People of God. I was so edified to learn that Bishop David Oakley, when he was Rector of Oscott College, arranged for the Life in the Spirit Seminars to be put on. It was an open invitation, and most of the seminarians attended. This is what we need and more.

There are so many misconceptions about Catholic Charismatic Renewal. A sound teaching on what this mainstream current of grace brings to the Church must surely be imparted to priests in training. Seminaries are sometimes places of resistance in this regard. When I was Diocesan Vocations Director, I was told by a more experienced Director that a man with a charismatic spirituality may well find it difficult in the seminary environment. What! I have heard of members of our parishes who have had a profound encounter with the Holy Spirit and their parish priest hasn't been able to assist them in their discipleship. Surely, this is wrong. How could that happen?

Healing ministry outside of the Sacraments, and what it has to offer the whole Church, is another core topic to be explored. Also, when I was in seminary, there was absolutely no discussion about spiritual warfare. No discussion about deliverance or exorcism. Really! That's why I learnt the hard way and on the hoof. Thank you Holy Spirit! Yes, if we keep close to Jesus, our hearts are well guarded. The grace of Ordination also counts for a great deal. However, there is a whole dimension which we all need to be particularly aware of. The priest is surely some-one who must understand this. People come to us with all sorts of issues. The greater understanding we have, and the more we have in the armoury, the more effective we will be. Jesus calls us to this task. The Holy Spirit is the Advocate.

ALL THE BAPTISED

Writing this as a priest, I would not want anyone to think that I am overlooking the priesthood of all the baptised. I have encouraged a reflection on our baptism in chapter 8, and all of this book is directed to the whole People of God. It is just that I felt that I was being asked to share these thoughts about my experience of my ordained priesthood.

I talked about the need for formation in seminaries around the Holy Spirit, the charismatic gifts and Charismatic Renewal. This is something that I believe needs to be on offer to all. An understanding and openness to healing prayer and healing ministry also need to be taught and encouraged. A solid catechesis around spiritual warfare and an understanding of deliverance ministry is essential. Those in training for the Permanent Diaconate; Pastoral Assistants; Catechists should be included. This is the Gospel. The Holy Spirit is the great gift to bring Jesus alive in our hearts and communities. We need that understanding and we need to call on all that God is putting at our disposal.

FOR REFLECTION AND DISCUSSION

What is your deepest desire?

Where do you see that you need more formation in the faith?

'You did not choose me but I chose you. And I appointed you to go out and bear fruit, fruit that will last' John 15:16
Reflect on this and discuss

How do you acknowledge your priesthood as a member of the People of God? Where does the Holy Spirit fit in?

Song: *However You Want* **by Jesus Culture**

25

Parishes
Alive in the Spirit

*'I have come that they may have life
and have it abundantly.'*
John 10:10

DIVINE RENOVATION

'I have a dream', exclaimed Martin Luther King in 1963 in
his famous speech calling for economic and civil rights and
an end to racism in the United States. 'I have a dream', he
says, and then goes on to outline what that looks like point
by point. A Gospel vision of freedom and justice for all. We
all need a dream. This is no different for a parish. We need
vision, inspired by the Holy Spirit, and a 'wish-list' of what
that vision might look like when fleshed out.

Over the past few years, Fr James Mallon has inspired
many parishes to consider the need for 'Divine
Renovation', through his book of the same title. His premise
is that we need to move from 'maintenance to mission'.
He describes parishes in the West as not being fit for
purpose. Catholic culture has been lost and our parish
structures haven't caught up. We're too busy maintaining
the status quo rather than focusing on the mission to
baptise and make disciples. Where in the past Catholic
Christians 'believed', 'behaved' and then 'belonged', this

model is the wrong way round for today's prevailing culture, he says. We need to engender a sense of 'belonging' in order to bring about 'believing' and then 'behaving'. We need to be intentional about all that we do. We need to build vision and so much more.

When I first read this book, I struggled to get past his analysis of our current situation. So accurate was it that it made me feel depressed. I wanted to bury my head in the sand despite a longing for something more. That is when a pure Holy Spirit moment happened. Caroline, who is now our Parish Outreach Worker, had come to deepened faith (hers is another story of the wonder of Jesus and the power of the Holy Spirit) and was getting more involved in the life of the parish. We would occasionally meet for some spiritual chats. As we met one day, shortly after I had properly read Fr Mallon's book, I felt the Holy Spirit say, 'Give her the book to read'. It was very clear. So, I asked her whether she would like to read it and see what she thought.

Well, it was less than 48 hours later that she got in touch with me. She had devoured the book and had come back with a whole load of thoughts and suggestions. I was really taken aback that she totally got everything being said, and could see exactly the points being made and the potential solution. I don't mean this to be patronising. I just thought there were certain nuances which would only be understood by those who have been wrestling with ministry and parishes for years. It was really of the Holy Spirit. She saw things exactly as I saw them, and had further insights and vision. I suddenly realised we were totally on the same wavelength. There was synergistic thinking going on. What was happening was pure gift. There was much of value for us to consider in this book, even if it seemed to apply to large, cash-rich, North American parishes.

AN HONEST ASSESSMENT

At the time of writing, I currently serve four parishes in South Bristol and Keynsham. When I first came to this part of the world, I was serving one parish. A few years later it became two and then four! We have come together as a 'Mission Area' under the banner of 'Called to More', a prophetic word shared by Caroline (see chapter 9). This has happened pretty rapidly under the clear direction of the Holy Spirit. Our vision for our parishes is, 'In the name of Jesus: Welcomed, Loved, Sent' and we seek to do all things with this in mind, bringing about a sense of belonging that gives people the space to come to deeper faith. Ultimately, we want to see people sent in the name of Jesus so that we are the evangelising community that we are called to be.

How are we getting on with this? Well, there is much to celebrate. We really have come a long way, and it would be so easy to overlook the extraordinary action of the Holy Spirit in our own lives and the life of all our parishes. It's always important to seek the positives and there are plenty of those. I am always uplifted by our liturgies in all the parishes. That is wonderful to experience as a priest.

Coming away, especially on a Sunday with that feeling of uplift; that sense of belonging; knowing that we've done our best to celebrate Jesus. It really is special.

There are also many good disciples in our parishes who have a passion for Jesus, expressed in many different ways. We have a good team of committed and supportive clergy and lay staff. We have many who offer their services in different ministries. As I reflect, there is so much to be thankful for. So much that brings joy and engenders hope. There is also so much that we don't see. We don't know how the seeds sown are flourishing as they are shared elsewhere. We are called to be beacons of hope as parishes and we can't always quantify the effect that has elsewhere. We simply trust that the Lord will bring those seeds to life. Yes, there's so much goodness in our parishes. I know what you're thinking – there's a 'but' coming!

In spite of the above, parish life is also really challenging, as it generally is everywhere. We are four smallish parishes. As with most parishes these days, there are lots of people who dip in and out of the life of the parish. I have really come to notice that parish is a pretty low priority for many people. COVID-19 hasn't helped here. During the pandemic we did all we could to reach out and keep in touch. COVID, though, seems to have been a watershed moment in which we have slipped further into decline as a result of not being proactive in making decisions about our structures at a Diocesan level. This is in spite of our coming together as a Mission Area. We struggle to build connections with young people and build up families. Let's face it, too, there is a lot of apathy around in general and it's a tough time in all areas of life and work.

There is a sense that for many in our parishes we are a service provider and parishioners are consumers. It is very difficult to find new people to 'step up' into ministry roles to serve our parishes. Commitment is a real issue. Roles once taken on by volunteers now require paid staff. When it comes to faith development, there seems to be a desire for it, but whenever we put courses on the take up is always low. We need to rethink how we are doing this. We need to think outside the box more in all respects. We need to let the Holy Spirit help us soar above and give us a new vision and renewed purpose.

It may be tempting for some who are reading this to think, 'Well, he's got a lot to say about the Holy Spirit but he's saying there isn't much fruit coming'. I'm not saying that. There is definitely fruit. I'm just being honest. I've been asked to write this book at this particular moment of my life and the life of these parishes. I simply believe there could be so much more. We are all 'Called to More' as our mission area motto goes. There is always more. What I say here is also what I know to be the experience of most parishes when they are really honest with themselves.

For me, it's as if there are clearly glowing embers which, if we allow the Holy Spirit to blow on them, will really ignite. That is why we need to invoke the Holy Spirit to fan into a flame the gifts within us, and to be open to so much on offer. That is why I am an advocate for baptism in the Holy Spirit. I have seen the difference it can make in the lives of so many. We need to create the environment for that to happen. So here is our wish-list for our parishes alive in the Holy Spirit.

WE HAVE A DREAM

♦   We dream of parishes alive in the Holy Spirit where all people are welcome and really come to know in their hearts that Jesus is Lord. Places of encounter with the living God. Places of genuine warmth and welcome, where our worship reflects our love of God. Places where we expect the Holy Spirit to show up.

♦   We dream of parishes alive in the Holy Spirit where we hunger for the Sacraments; parishes where we are confident in approaching the altar and knowing this is Jesus who gives himself for us; parishes where we adore Jesus Christ in the Blessed Sacrament.

♦   We dream of parishes alive in the Holy Spirit where the Word of God underpins our lives. Where we are confident of Jesus speaking to our hearts.

♦   We dream of parishes alive in the Holy Spirit where we become solid evangelising communities, diffusing far and wide the name of Jesus. Parishes where we desire to get out of our buildings for the sake of reaching out. Where maintenance is focused on enabling mission.

♦   We dream of parishes alive in the Holy Spirit where

the principles of Charismatic Renewal are embedded. Where the gifts of the Holy Spirit are not seen as something separate, or extra, but as essential to our mission. Where the flourishing of the graces of our Baptism and Confirmation can happen, and fresh outpourings of the Holy Spirit can be expected.

♦ We dream of parishes alive in the Holy Spirit where we offer regular healing prayer as a sign of love, and where we are expectant of signs and wonders.

♦ We dream of parishes alive in the Holy Spirit where people 'pray in the Spirit at all times in every prayer and supplication' (Eph 6:18) and where this is reflected in our worship.

♦ We dream of parishes alive in the Holy Spirit which empower lay people in their vocation, and give them ownership over their own formation. Where missionary disciples are nourished and sent in Jesus' name in the power of the Holy Spirit.

♦ We dream of parishes alive in the Holy Spirit where we build a solid ministry to young people and families, assisting them in their discipleship and helping them to discern their vocation.

♦ We dream of parishes alive in the Holy Spirit where we develop a deep culture of loving service, reaching out especially to those in need.

♦ We dream of parishes alive in the Holy Spirt where we always ask the question, 'How does this serve the Lord?

How does this build others up? How does this share the Gospel?'

Sometimes it's good to dream big!
We need to be aspirational.

Writing this book is a good moment for our parishes to reflect on all of this and move forward in hope. Surely this wish-list is simply God's wish for all his children. This is who we are, and we just need the help of the Holy Spirit to come to know God's promise for us fully.

I have shared our parish prayer earlier in this book. I finish with another Spirit-filled prayer:

Come Holy Spirit, come!
Come like a mighty wind!
Come breathe new life in all areas of our lives.
Come strengthen us in Your love and guide us into truth.
Come fill our hearts, our homes, our parish.
Come, Holy Spirit, come!
Confirm within us the Father's love
and draw us ever closer to Jesus.
Purify our hearts and help us to discern
that which is true, good and holy.
Fix our eyes on heavenly things
and give us a new thirst for You.
Transform us and burn away
all that keeps us from following You.
Come, Holy Spirit, come!

Stir up in us a joyful faith
and waken in us the graces of baptism.
Give us eyes of mercy and compassion
and help us recognise those in need.
Raise us up and equip us to be
courageous witnesses to the Gospel.
Bless us and send us out as channels
of God's love, hope and healing.
Amen.
(from the Parish of St Peter and the Winchester Martyrs)

FOR REFLECTION AND DISCUSSION

What is your dream for yourself; your family; our world?

What is your dream for our parishes? How can the Holy Spirit assist with this?

Are you invoking the Holy Spirit more? Are you desirous of flourishing in the gifts of the Holy Spirit?

Song: *Alive Again* by Matt Maher

26

Mary and
the Holy Spirit

'The angel said to her,
The Holy Spirit will come upon you,
and the power of the Most High
will overshadow you.'
Luke 1:35

THE ANNUNCIATION

Oh, how I love that scene of the Annunciation in Franco Zeffirelli's *Jesus of Nazareth*. It is very much in my heart. I watched the film in Lent 2000 not long after my rediscovery and full acknowledgement of Jesus in my life. I found it incredibly moving. Well, why wouldn't it be? It is doing its best to imagine the most profound encounter in the whole of human history. For me, the thought that went into this scene was surely inspired by the Holy Spirit. Certainly the Holy Spirit speaks to me through it.

The scene begins with Mary asleep. She is awoken by the sound of the wooden shutter to her sleeping quarter being blown open and clattering against the wall. Light streams into the room. A gentle breeze falls upon her. She looks up towards the light in the window and suddenly recoils in fright to the back of her room, knocking over a pot. She quickly gathers herself and edges forward towards the light asking, 'Who are you?' Now in the fullness of the light entering the window, she stands prayerfully attentive. 'How can that be? No man has ever touched me?' She continues to listen to the apparent silence and then slowly drops to her knees. The light now shines all around her. The breeze gently blows her hair. 'Behold the handmaiden of the Lord', she says. 'Be it done unto me according to your word'.

It's the breeze that really gets me in this scene. It is evocative of the Breath; the Spirit hovering over the water at the beginning of creation as described in the first chapter of Genesis. Mary is the new creation. The Holy Spirit is hovering over her to bring about heaven in her. She is to be the mother of Jesus Christ, the Eternal Word. She is to become the true Ark of the Covenant; the New Eve, who will always point away from herself to the Saviour to be born from her. Prepared for this most exalted of vocations by receiving the merits of her Son's death and resurrection at the moment of her conception, she will be the Mother of the Church and the model disciple. The Annunciation is the encounter of all encounters. Mary becomes God-bearer.

How can it be? How can it be? 'The Holy Spirit will come upon you'. The mission of the Holy Spirit, Lord, giver of Life, is coterminous with the Word. The Holy Spirit sanctifies the womb of Mary and brings about life within. I have been privileged enough to visit the Basilica of the Annunciation in Nazareth, and within there is a house which tradition maintains was where Mary lived. On the altar in front of the ruins in the lower part of the basilica are written the words, 'The Word became Flesh here'. The Holy Spirit brought about the will of the Trinity in bringing God into space and time, inserting God into the womb of a peasant girl who consented to the greatest of callings.

THE HOLY SPIRIT IN MARY'S LIFE

I haven't left Mary to last as an afterthought. It was my desire to begin this book with the great proclamation of 'Jesus is Lord'. Mary would always want us to shout that truth from the rooftops. She doesn't want us to be looking at her. 'Do whatever he tells you' (John 2:5), she says. However, we can't get away from the fact that our Lord gave us Mary as our mother (John 19:26-27). It would be disobedient to ignore that. I feel blessed that my mum is still alive. I know she prays for me. Even when she does go to God, I believe she will still pray for me. The thing about Mary is that her place in heaven is clearly defined. She is the Queen of Heaven. She is a wonderful intercessor. She pleads on our behalf just like our earthly mothers, but within the halls of heaven.

The Holy Spirit is abundantly present in the encounter with Mary and Elizabeth (Luke 1:39-57). Mary is full of the Holy Spirit and when she greets Elizabeth, Elizabeth in turn is filled with the Holy Spirit. John leaps in her womb, showered by the Holy Spirit. Prophecy issues from the lips of Elizabeth, and Mary praises God with further prophetic words. After John's birth, Zechariah's temporarily bound up tongue is loosened (Luke 1:67-79). He is filled with the Holy Spirit and answers the questions of the neighbours in the form of a prophetic prayer of praise. Then, after the birth of Jesus, as Mary brings the Christ child to the temple, Simeon, on whom the Holy Spirit had already been acting, also prophesies as he recognises the light of the world (Luke 2:25-32).

All in and around Mary is the presence and action of the Holy Spirit. She was also there at Pentecost. Lest we forget, it was not just the disciples who were there. Mary was there with other women and men (Acts 1:12:14). The difference with the others gathered at Pentecost is that they didn't know the Holy Spirit. Mary, however, had been possessed by the Holy Spirit from the first moment of her existence. She always did the Lord's bidding, and finally the Holy Spirit overshadowed her so that she would conceive within her the Lord and Saviour of all. It is for this reason that Mary is sometimes referred to as the Spouse of the Holy Spirit. There is a special union between Mary and the Holy Spirit. The marriage union is surely a good analogy for such a bond.

Mary leads us to Christ. Mary always points to Jesus. It just so happens that God decided that Mary was called to be involved in the mystery of our redemption. It just so happens that we are clearly shown through the Word of God that we are Mary's children. She is our mother. That is God's will. Don't be afraid of showing your devotion for her as she will keep turning you to her Son.

In our walk of discipleship let us keep our eyes firmly on

Jesus. He is our Saviour. Let us remember that we have friends in the Communion of Saints praying for us; not least Mary, Mother of the Church. Let us remember that Mary gives a wonderful and perfect example of openness to the Holy Spirit.

FOR REFLECTION AND DISCUSSION

Where does Mary fit into your life?

Can you see the intimate connection between Mary and the Holy Spirit?

Reflect on some of the images from St Luke in this chapter. Share your thoughts with others.

Why not ask Mary to pray for you for a fresh release of the gifts of the Holy Spirit.

Song: *Dance With Me* by Jesus Culture

27

Next Steps

'Repent, and be baptised every one of you
in the name of Jesus Christ so that your sins
may be forgiven; and you will receive the Holy Spirit.
For the promise is for you, for your children,
and for all who are far away, everyone
whom the Lord our God calls to him.'
Acts 2:38:39

AN INVITATION
Well, that was a rollercoaster and I barely scratched the surface!

I simply want to make the point that, when we follow Jesus and draw close, it is the Holy Spirit who is making it happen. The Holy Spirit, whom Jesus with the Father sent out across the whole earth and throughout the universe. The Holy Spirit is the fulness of God. There is always more. We need to allow the graces of our Baptism and Confirmation to be released within us so that we can more confidently stand up and proclaim, 'Jesus is Lord'.

Just as I was finishing this book, Pat, who I mentioned in chapter 5 as a prophet for baptism in the Holy Spirit, handed me a word. She had received it one morning and

I believe it is to be shared. It is relevant to this book and I want to share it here.

My dear children,
I want you to know there is so much more to Christianity and life in general. You see Baptism and Confirmation aren't enough. We all need a living experience of the love of God who wants us to experience the fullness of life. Only with the empowering of the Holy Spirit can that truly happen!

Jesus came that we might live life to the full. He came to set us free from all that would prevent that happening. He died that we might live. By dying, rising and ascending into Heaven, He was able to send His Holy Spirit not just at Pentecost but for all time to come. The most precious gift we could ever have. The important thing is we have to ask and accept this gift with a sincere heart. Please don't wait any longer. Life is too precious.

WHAT NEXT?

In 2021, Pope Francis encouraged all those involved with Catholic Charismatic Renewal to *'share baptism in the Holy Spirit with everyone in the Church'*. He encouraged parishes to put Life in the Spirit Seminars on. Different events take place in parishes up and down the country seeking to lead people forward in their faith and to be open to the gifts of the Holy Spirit and the grace of baptism in the Holy Spirit. These events are often linked to Diocesan

Charismatic Renewal teams. COVID-19, naturally, has had an effect on these gatherings and they have dwindled. Hopefully they will start to flourish again soon. These diocesan teams are linked in to a national body with close contact to the Bishops' Conference of England and Wales. I would recommend looking at the Catholic Charismatic Renewal website (www.ccr.org.uk) for more details and lots of useful information.

It is always good to have the support of others on our journey but we don't all have that benefit. There may not be Life in the Spirit Seminars or other events happening close to you. There are useful resources in the next section, such as 'The Gift', produced by CaFE (Catholic Faith Exploration), available as download or DVD, which you may like to watch on your own or with a group. 'The Gift' is a filmed Life in the Spirit course with excellent speakers and reflection questions.

In spite of the above, if you are moved to act on what you have read and are seeking a release of the gifts of the Holy Spirit; if you are desirous of being baptised in the Holy Spirit, just as Pope Francis and Pope Benedict have encouraged, then prepare yourself well and ask! Here's a way in:

♦ Make a good examination of conscience.

♦ Seek forgiveness - use the Sacrament of Reconciliation as the supreme way of receiving the assurance of God's forgiveness if you are able to.

♦   In a heartfelt manner, make a renewal of your profession of faith:

> *I reject Satan.*
> *And all his works.*
> *And all his empty promises.*
> *I believe in God the Father Almighty, creator of heaven and earth.*
> *I believe in Jesus Christ, his only Son, our Lord, who was born of the Virgin Mary, was crucified, died and was buried, rose from the dead, and is now seated at the right hand of the Father.*
> *I believe in the Holy Spirit,*
> *the holy catholic Church,*
> *the communion of saints,*
> *the forgiveness of sins,*
> *the resurrection of the body*
> *and life everlasting.*

Then, in faith, pray with an expectant heart with hands open in a gesture of receiving:

> **Dear Lord Jesus,**
> **I renounce Satan and all my sinful ways that keep me separated from you. I thank you for dying on the cross in order to save me from my sins and with your resurrection, you bring me to new life in you. I wish to surrender myself to you and follow you as the Lord of my heart. I ask you to baptise me in the Holy**

Spirit and in power, that I might follow you more closely and love you more deeply all the days of my life. Let the gifts of the Holy Spirit come alive in me. In your precious name I pray. Amen!

Start to look out for signs of how life is changing in and around you. Keep up that deep awareness of the love of God for you in Jesus Christ and remember to **keep invoking the Holy Spirit.**

Be assured of my prayers. Be assured of the prayers of all the People of God on your behalf!

www.dftholyspirit.com

Useful Resources

CaFE *(Catholic Faith Exploration)* resources, such as 'The Gift – A Life in the Spirit Course' can be found at www.faithcafe.org

I recommend the following books which are available from Goodnews Books and give a solid grounding for understanding the grace of baptism in the Holy Spirit:

Catechism of the Catholic Church
CTS Revised Edition (2021)
Naturally, the Catechism is replete with deep insights into the Person of the Holy Spirit. It is essential reading.
CCC 683-744 gives the chief focus on the article of faith, 'I believe in the Holy Spirit'.

Baptism in the Holy Spirit
International Catholic Charismatic Renewal Services Doctrinal Commission.
This is an excellent document looking into the foundations of this essential grace in Scripture and the Catholic tradition. It gives the necessary theological framework for baptism in the Holy Spirit.

Towards a Fuller Life in the Holy Spirit
Charles Whitehead (2011)
Charles writes in such an accessible style but with the authority of huge experience of Catholic Charismatic Renewal across the world. He has written many books but this is a good primer.

Divine Renovation
Fr James Mallon (2014)
A must read for all ministering in parishes. There is great insight and so much of value here.

The Holy Spirit and an Evolving Church
James A. Coriden (2017)
A really accessible book examining the indispensable role of the Holy Spirit from the early Church to today.

www.dftholyspirit.com

DON'T FORGET THE HOLY SPIRIT

*Further copies of this book
can be obtained from*

*Goodnews Books
St. John's Church Complex
296 Sundon Park Road
Luton, Beds. LU3 3AL*

*www.goodnewsbooks.co.uk
orders@goodnewsbooks.co.uk
01582 571011*